Inside the Cook County Jail

C.J. Wilkinson

Copyright © 2019 C.J. Wilkinson
All rights reserved
First Edition

PAGE PUBLISHING, INC.
New York, NY

First originally published by Page Publishing, Inc. 2019

ISBN 978-1-64462-520-0 (Paperback)
ISBN 978-1-64462-521-7 (Digital)

Printed in the United States of America

In loving memory to my grandmother,
Carmela M. Key

INSIDE THE COOK COUNTY JAIL

The call came in about the robbery, and we had to respond immediately.

When we arrived at the bank, the two suspects were just exiting the building with their guns drawn. Dropping down behind our car, we announced that we were deputy sheriffs from the Cook County Sheriffs Department and told them to drop their guns and put their hands in the air. The two suspects started firing at us, leaving us no alternative but to fire back.

I was scared stiff; what should I do? This was the first time I had ever been faced with this type of situation. My next thought was to try to think logically about how to get the situation under control. I looked to my partners for some sort of answer to this problem, and what we came up with was to try to surround the two suspects and force them to surrender. We finally got them to surrender, but not until one of our officers was shot.

Luckily for our officer, it was only a flesh wound, and he was treated at one of the outpatient care centers and then released within a couple of hours.

The two assailants were arrested and charged with robbery and attempted murder of a police officer. They were both found guilty in court and sentenced to eight years in the state penitentiary in Joliet, Illinois.

PROLOGUE

Inmates come in many different sizes, shapes, races, ages, and personalities. Some of the inmates who were locked up were truly innocent, and then there were the ones who were as guilty as sin.

There were inmates in jail for crimes that range from petty theft, all the way up to the more serious crimes: rape, robbery, murder, drug possession, child molestation, criminal trespass to businesses as well as homes, arson, and weapons violations.

Inmates come from all walks of life. Some were successful businesspeople; some were homeless people. The main trait they all had in common was the fact that they had all lost respect for themselves as well as everyone else.

Their lives now consist of being told when and how to do everything that they once had the freedom to do on their own. Things that they once took for granted: waking up when they wanted to, watching whatever they wanted on TV, eating what they wanted at the time they wanted to, showering when they wanted to, spending time with their families—all these were now privileges. But most of all, they had lost their freedom.

CHAPTER 1

Officer Meets Inmates

As I entered the old building at the Cook County Jail in Chicago, Illinois, because of my petite size, my heart leaped into my throat as I took in the surroundings. Totally in awe, my brown eyes bulged as I joined two hundred other men and women as they entered the roll call room. I felt a bit out of place; I appeared to be the only light-skinned female in the room. I was so nervous that I started running my long fingernails through my medium-length blond hair.

The captain, lieutenant, and sergeant of the division that I was assigned to introduced themselves, adopting a very militant demeanor. They came across as very intimidating to me as they were all tall, husky men with clean-shaven faces and deep voices.

The closer they got, alphabetically, to calling my name for duty assignment, the more anxious I became. I couldn't fathom what lay ahead of me once I reached my destination. The anticipation continued to build, reaching its peak when the captain called my name for dorm I–J of Division Six. I answered in a loud voice, "Here, sir," and then slowly walked down the long gray corridor leading to the dorm.

When I reached my assignment, I stood in the doorway for a couple of minutes to look around. The dorm had two levels, an upper and a lower. There were eleven cells on each level, housing two inmates per cell.

The dayroom was located in the middle of the dorm. It contained four large metal tables bolted to the floor, for the inmates to eat at. Located in the center of the room, bolted high on the wall, was a television set.

I slowly entered the dorm to make a count of all the inmates housed there. The first thing I noticed was the stench of body odor and mustiness in the air. I hesitated for a moment before ascending the stairs to the upper level. With each step I took toward the top of the staircase, I could feel my heart beating harder and harder until it seemed it would burst through my chest. Slowly walking the length of the cells, I counted the inmates on both levels. After counting the inmates' ID cards, I called the count into the security office. While waiting for the count to clear, I thought about how I would handle the dorm's activities during my eight-hour tour of duty.

The announcement came that the count was clear; the day shift was now leaving, and I was on my own. What a scary feeling that was for me; although I made sure not to let the inmates see my fear.

I opened the cell doors with the buttons on the control panel in the inner lock. I had to laugh to myself when the inmates left their cells and immediately came into the dayroom to check out the new female officer. They all acted like they had never seen a female before.

I was a little intimidated by the inmates as they were all very muscular and had stern expressions on their faces.

Dinner was served at 4:30 p.m. sharp. All the inmates lined up in a single-file line while the trays were brought into the dayroom and stacked on one of the tables in the dorm. No inmate was supposed to take a tray until all trays had been counted by the dorm officer. Inmates assigned as workers were the only ones allowed to enter and exit the dorms. They bring in the food and beverages for the other inmates and then pick up the empty trays and milk crates about an hour later. If any clean clothes, linens, or other items were needed for any inmate on the dorm, the officer must call for a worker to bring them to the dorm.

Church services were held at 6:00 p.m. in the chapel. Most of the inmates attended just so they could get out of their dorms to visit with other inmates in their divisions as well as give or get cigarettes and/or drugs. As I took down the names and numbers of the inmates who wanted to attend church, I heard them making snide and suggestive comments about my looks and the proportions of my figure. I was very angered by their crude comments. I was very glad when the inmates had left for church, and I could sit back and relax for a few minutes. This was harder than I had originally thought it would be: more in the mental capacity than the physical at this time.

The inmates returned to the dorm an hour later. Most of them were all wired up and rowdy. I had to tell them several times to quiet down, or they would all have to go to their cells for the remainder of the night. Of course, none of them wanted to be confined in their cells, so they were accommodating.

Shortly after all the inmates were signed back in from church, Nurse Buckner, a young dark-skinned man with a medium build, arrived at the dorm to pass out medication to the inmates. All the inmates lined up in a single-file line approximately two feet from the medication cart. Nurse Buckner called each inmate up to the cart one by one. Some of the inmates would get medication so they could trade it to other inmates for food, cigarettes, or drugs at a later time.

An inmate named Carlos, a tall, rough-looking man with broad shoulders, tried to hide his medication in the palm of his hand. I saw what he had done and told him he would have to take the medication right now, or I would take it from him. Carlos became very indignant, using his broad shoulders to intimidate me. He said that if I tried to take the medication from him, he would knock me out. I hesitated a moment, thinking what a big inmate he was and then becoming alarmed by the rough look he had in his bold brown eyes. I hoped that he wouldn't put up a fight.

I told all the inmates to go to their cells so I could isolate Carlos from the rest of the inmates to prevent any further problems. I called for my supervisor, Sergeant Baily, to come to the dorm.

For a short, stocky man, Baily had quite a temper. His anger showed in his green eyes as he had Carlos removed from the dorm and put in isolation. All inmates were put in isolation when they didn't follow the rules of the jail.

After Nurse Buckner finished passing out the medication, I had to write the report on the incident. As I wrote the report, thoughts went through my head about what might have happened if Carlos had been out of control. What if he would have just hit me? How would I have handled the situation then? I had a really eerie feeling in my stomach. The reality of the job was sinking in.

By the time I had finished the report and turned it over to my sergeant, it was time to lock up all the cells for the night and make a final count of the inmates. I had an officer to back me up whenever I needed to enter the dorm. Officer Franks was working the dorm directly across the hall, so I called him to assist me. Once he arrived at my dorm, I took the keys for the cells and went inside. I felt safe with him there as he was a largely built man with huge callused hands.

Once again, those stairs looked very scary to me as I started to ascend them. This time, it didn't take me as long to reach the top. I felt a little more secure in my ability to lock up without any problems. Little did I know what lay ahead of me. As I was locking the cells on the upper level, an inmate named Juan, with a medium build and a very big chip on his shoulder, approached me and patted me on the ass. I spun around and slapped Juan across his broad face and asked him what the hell he thought he was doing.

It didn't take long for the other inmates on the upper level to become aware of the commotion. George and Wilton, the two inmates from cell five, came running out of their cell and grabbed Juan. After beating Juan up, bouncing him off walls and then throwing him into his cell, George and Wilton smiled at me and told me they were sure that Juan was ready for lock up now. I thanked them for their assistance and told them to return to their cell for the count. They returned to their cell without incident.

As I finished locking up the cells, I thought. *If I had seen two huge and mean-looking inmates running toward me, I would have returned to my cell as quickly as possible.* I then went down to the lower level to lock up the cells and make a count of the inmates. Fortunately for me, there were no more incidents.

After returning to the interlock, I spoke to Officer Franks about what had happened on the upper level. I wanted to know if I should notify my sergeant and write a report on the incident. He told me that since the situation was taken care of, I shouldn't worry about it anymore.

Now that all the inmates were locked in their cells, I sat at my desk and wrote all of the evening's events in my logbook. Once I had completed that and counted all the inmate ID cards, I was able to breathe a sigh of relief. I realized that things could have been a lot worse. I was going home in one piece and had made it through my first night at the Cook County Jail. Boy, was I relieved. I knew my family would be glad to see me too.

Carlos was let out of isolation and returned to his jail cell just before the count cleared, and I was leaving to go home.

CHAPTER 2

Accident of Murder

My husband, Ken, six foot two, weighing 230 pounds, has broad shoulders and a stocky build. He also works at the Cook County Jail. He works in Division One, a maximum-security area of the jail for inmates who were waiting trial for crimes of a very serious nature: murder, rape, drug possession and sales, child molestation, and battery with a deadly weapon. The conditions Ken had to work in were very dirty, rat-infested, and unsafe. Most of the equipment didn't work properly. Cells didn't lock, which meant that the inmates housed in those cells were never locked up when they should have been. This gave them access to the telephone after hours. A lot of the inmates whose cells didn't lock were members of gangs, and that was when they would make their phone calls to their other gang members.

Ken's night at the jail started out like any other, taking the 3:00 p.m. count of the inmates and their ID cards, calling in the count and waiting for the count to clear.

On this particular night, though, things ended very tragically for an inmate named Robert, a.k.a. "Puny." He was five foot eleven with a husky build and carried himself in an intelligent manner. Robert was the chief shot-caller on dorm 1F, so he would always tell the other inmates what he wanted them to do and when he wanted them to do it. Most of the inmates did what he asked because they were afraid of him. If they refused to obey Puny, they would be punished (more commonly referred to as a "violation") by him or one of the gang members he designated. The violations were in the form of beatings, loss of phone privileges, loss of food for an indefinite amount of time, loss of personal possessions, and rape. The most commonly used form was the rape. Any inmate who tried to fight back during his violation would be violated a second time. Most of the inmates found that it was best to just take their violation and not say anything about it or try to stop it. That way, when it was over, things went back to the way they were before the violation took place.

Puny was in charge of all the violations with the inmates; no one else in the dorm was authorized to carry them out. He was the gang member who was respected the most mainly because he was feared by the other inmates on his dorm as well as inmates from other dorms.

Puny also had a very bad drug habit: one that would have cost most inmates a lot of money. But he knew how to get whatever he wanted from whoever he wanted it from. This included certain officers, sergeants, lieutenants, and members of the medical staff from the division he was in as well as some from other divisions. Also, being a barber gave him freedom of movement throughout the division. Puny's favorite drug to use was heroin; in fact, that was what ended up killing him.

When Ken left on his lunch break about 6:00 p.m., an officer named Branowski came to the dorm as his relief. Branowski was a chubby man with short hair that accentuated his bloodshot eyes. Rumor had it that Officer Branowski had been bringing in drugs to various inmates throughout the division. He would get money from them in exchange for the drugs he would bring in. Sometimes, he would bring in other things for the inmates such as cigarettes, food, lighters, batteries for their portable radios, and dice so they could gamble. While Ken was gone to lunch, Officer Branowski gave Puny a syringe and some heroin.

Puny took it back to his cell to prepare to shoot it into a vein in his arm. He used a spoon and a lighter to cook the heroin, after which he filled the syringe. At about 6:45 p.m., Puny stuck the needle into his arm and shot the drugs into his vein. Unfortunately for him, it was a lethal dose, and he died before he could even take the needle out of his arm.

Ken returned to the dorm at approximately 7:00 p.m. When he entered the dorm to make a count of the inmates, he didn't see Puny sitting in the corner of the dayroom where he usually sat. Ken was very suspicious and decided to go back to the cell area. There, he saw Puny lying on the floor next to his bunk with a needle hanging out of his arm. Ken was sickened by what he saw as well as being a bit in shock. He had only been with the county for a little more than a month. He yelled for an officer to come and help him with Puny; ironically, it was Officer Branowski who arrived at the dorm. When Ken told him what had happened and that he had to call his supervisor, Sergeant Williamson, to come to the dorm and investigate what had happened, Officer Branowski became very nervous.

Sergeant Williamson, a large-framed man, who was as loud as he was big, arrived on the dorm and was informed of the incident. He then notified the investigations department and called for a member of the medical staff to come to the dorm. Sergeant Williamson believed in going strictly by the book; in fact, he was one of the few sergeants who had really earned his stripes through hard work.

Before the medical staff or investigators arrived, two inmates, Brady and Anton, both with dark complexions and showing the signs of long-term drug abuse arrived, and since they were friends of Puny and wanted to try to save him from dying of an overdose, decided to remove the needle from his arm. They then took Puny out of his cell and brought him into the shower stall and turned on the cold water in hopes of reviving him. No luck, though. Puny was already dead; no one and nothing could save him now.

Paramedic Watson, a short, wiry man with frizzy hair and dark skin, arrived on the dorm a few minutes before the investigators. After he took Puny's pulse and other vital signs, getting a negative reading on all of them, he told the sergeant that Puny was dead. Nevertheless, days later, reports stated that the inmate was alive when he was removed from the jail. According to a spokesperson for the sheriff's department, no inmate has ever died in the jail then or at any time before this incident. What a crock of shit that was!

When Investigator Waters, a tall and slender man with dark hair and eyes, and Investigator Green, a tall, husky man with a black patch over his left eye, arrived at the dorm, they ordered Ken to perform a complete and thorough search of Puny's cell. He did as he was told but later found that you never touch anything at the scene of a crime until a complete investigation has been done by the police. The crime scene had already been tampered with by the two inmates housed on the same dorm, Brady and Anton.

Originally the incident was referred to as an accident. Later, after the autopsy had been performed and part of the needle had been found in Puny's arm, they changed it to an unintentional overdose. In actuality, it should have been called murder.

Ken was questioned by both investigators. He was also questioned by the coroner, Ralph Holmes, an elderly man with gray hair and by an investigator from the Chicago Police Department named Boswell Trudy. Trudy was a man of medium height with intriguing blue eyes. Ken was questioned repeatedly until they were all satisfied with his answers.

Several inmates on the dorm were also questioned by the investigators and the coroner. Questions such as "Where were you when Puny shot up the heroin?" "Did you see who gave Puny the drugs or the syringe?" "Were there any other inmates or officers on the dorm while Officer Wilkinson was gone to lunch?"

By the time they had all finished questioning Ken and going over the incident with his supervisor, Sergeant Williamson wrote up the report of what had taken place; it was three thirty in the morning.

Ken was exhausted as well as being very stressed out from the day's events, the long hours he had already worked, lack of sleep, and just frustration in general.

CHAPTER 3

Negligence or Cover-Up

The death of Puny in Division One was laid to rest for months before anyone did anything about the allegations of it being murder. Finally, Ken talked to an inmate he knew who could tell him why Puny was given the lethal dose of heroin.

Cyprus, a short, dumpy-looking man with red curly hair and a pimpled complexion, told Ken that Puny had crossed another inmate in a rival gang. This made many of the gang members angry at Puny. As a result, there was a hit put on him. Whenever a hit was put out on an inmate, it was usually carried out within a very short span of time. In Puny's case, though, it took a few months to carry out because of him being one of the chief shot-callers and because none of the gang chiefs traveled alone. Chiefs usually tried to stay in groups of three or more gang members, especially when any kind of threat had been made against one of them. Cyprus was one of the inmates who stayed close to Puny as well as some of the other gang chiefs throughout the jail. Unfortunately for Puny, they couldn't protect him from being killed.

Cyprus told Ken how upset he was about Puny being murdered. Puny was more than just another gang member to him; they had been very close friends for many years. The two met on the streets when they were in their early teens. They got into trouble together as well as having good times together.

Ken asked Cyprus to explain to him what had led up to the murder of Puny. All Cyprus could remember was that he and Puny had gotten into a verbal altercation with an inmate named Tyler over Tyler's woman. Tyler was a tall, slender man with a scruffy beard and mustache. Apparently, Puny had been seeing Tyler's girlfriend before he was locked up. (Tyler had already been in jail for about six months by the time Puny went to jail.) Tyler was pissed off at Puny, as the main rule among gangs is: never mess with each other's women or children. Puny didn't follow his own rules, and that ended up being a fatal mistake on his part.

Ken wrote another report containing the new information he received regarding Puny's death and addressed it to his supervisor, Sergeant Williamson. Ken then notified investigations of the new information. In keeping with the county's policy that no inmate ever died in jail, the paperwork got buried. By who? We'll never know. Ken waited a month, and when nothing was done about the new information, he decided to try another avenue. He contacted a member of the union to see what could be done about the situation. Unfortunately, that was another dead end as the union didn't want to get involved.

Ken then tried to contact one of the original investigators who had handled the incident the night that Puny died. Ken reached another dead end there as well; both of the investigators had been fired shortly after the night of Puny's death. Neither of the investigators handled the investigation properly. Ken thought the reason they were fired was to cover up facts that could have proven that Puny was murdered. Without the two of them in the way, the evidence could be disposed of without any suspicions.

The last avenue that Ken tried was to call the news media to see if maybe they could put some heat on the sheriff's department. He hoped that the media would let the truth be known. All allegations were totally denied and the case was put to rest once again.

Ken and Cyprus talked again about what had happened the night Puny died. Each wished he could have done more. They both realized, however, that nothing they could do now would bring Puny back.

It became apparent that the county didn't care about the truth; all they cared about was not looking bad in the public eye. Security and safety for officers as well as inmates were always supposed to be the primary concern. Too bad the county doesn't agree with that.

Ken found with each passing day that he had to look out for himself because no one else would. It was a real shame when you can't count on your coworkers or your supervisors to back you up when you try to do your job the way it was meant to be done. Working in law enforcement was hard enough, without having to fight your coworkers and supervisors at the same time. It was to be expected that officers would have to fight inmates occasionally, but why must officers have to fight each other?

This was just one example of how, when an inmate dies in jail, it gets buried under all the politics of the system. Right or wrong, one officer alone cannot change the system no matter how hard he or she tries.

Ken stayed in Division One for about nine months before he went into the training academy. Once he had finished with his training, he transferred to another division in the hopes that things would be different.

CHAPTER 4

Academy: Training or Torture

Every person who works for the Cook County Department of Corrections has to attend a twelve-week training academy before they were considered to be at the rank of an officer.

Most of us went into the academy within the first year of being with the county, although some had to wait longer, and some went in earlier than the year.

The subjects of study consisted of first-response medical training, correctional law, report writing, and firearms training. In addition, we studied stress management, riot control, US jail standards-rules and regulations, self-defense, and the proper procedures for making an arrest. First-response consisted of learning CPR, the basics of first aid, gathering information at the scene of an accident, keeping the victim as calm and quiet as possible, as well as trying to find out as much about the victim's medical background as possible so that they could be treated as soon as humanly possible.

Paramedic Young had a lot of enthusiasm when he taught. He was a thirty-five-year-old man with a slightly large build. His dark hair shimmered like a light, and his dark eyes glowed when he told us about the last fifteen years he had spent as a paramedic. All the lives he saved, babies he delivered, and accidents he had seen left him with mixed emotions.

There was an inflatable doll called Annie that was used for CPR training. This way, if we made any mistakes, we wouldn't hurt a real person. Annie was a real sport. One incident that really stands out in my mind was when we had to save a victim from an area that was on fire and then revive her. Annie didn't make it through too many of the fires without getting scorched, but by the end of the training, she had recovered nicely.

We had to wear face masks with the front blacked out as if we were in a smoke-filled room. We had to feel around for any bodies that might be trapped in the building that was on fire.

Everyone had to perform first aid on at least three people during the course, plus take four written exams and pass them with at least 70 percent on each of them. I managed to score a 92 percent in the class.

The next part of our training dealt with correctional law. Our instructor was an attorney named Mr. Mongella. Although he was an elderly man with graying hair, he had a very energetic way of teaching his course. Attorney Mongella made sure that everyone read different chapters in the law books, answered questionnaires, attended one court trial for a murder case, and passed three written exams on constitutional law as well as the different crime classifications and the length of sentences.

In the court case we attended, the defendant was a nineteen-year-old Hispanic man named Enrico. He was charged with using a knife, along with his medium-sized build, to overpower, rob, and kill a small-boned, elderly woman who was eighty-two years old and half-blind. The victim, Ms. Cautery, lived in a retirement home not far from where Enrico lived. He broke into her room late in the evening and told her that he wanted all her money. He then told her that he wouldn't hurt her if she cooperated with him. Ms. Cautery only had $200 in her room, which angered Enrico to the point that he stabbed her twenty-five times, causing her death.

During the trial, we were shown pictures of the victim's stab wounds, and we listened to evidence from the attorneys for the defense and the prosecution.

Defense Attorney Adams, a young man with light hair and blue eyes, had been in practice for only five years. He stated that his client Enrico was not in control of his faculties at the time of the murder because of his addiction to cocaine. He wanted us to believe that

Enrico had been so out of control because of his heavy drug usage that he couldn't be held responsible for his actions.

On the other hand, prosecuting Attorney Bonner, an elderly man with dark hair and eyes, who had been in practice for almost twenty years, stated that Enrico knew exactly what he was doing when he robbed and stabbed Ms. Cautery to death. The evidence he presented was that Enrico was sufficiently in control of himself so as to take a knife, go over to Ms. Cautery's home, break in, and then demand money from her before stabbing her to death.

Judge Franklin sentenced Enrico to twenty years in jail without any chance of parole. (In reality, he would actually serve thirteen years of his sentence.)

Report writing was the next course of study.

The instructor we had was named Ms. Samuels. She was a middle-aged woman with reddish hair pulled back off her face to accentuate her bright blue eyes. She had a real talent for getting everyone involved in the class. We had several reading assignments, three written tests, two skits to perform, and two skits to watch and write a report on. One of the skits we watched was about two inmates named Blake and Harvey who got into a fight over a dinner tray. It started out with both inmates in a line waiting for their dinner trays. Suddenly, Blake hit Harvey in the back of the head and said he was going to take Harvey's tray as soon as he sat down to eat. Harvey told Blake to go fuck himself. After the skit was completed, we were all asked to write a report on what had just taken place. It was pretty ironic that almost every one of us had a different perception of what had happened. Yet all of us had viewed the same thing.

When we went through the firearms training, we had three instructors. The first, Mr. Darin, a young man in his early thirties, was a very big help to a lot of the people who had never shot a gun before. His easygoing disposition, along with his clear blue eyes, always made you feel at ease when he was talking to you, especially if you were afraid of your weapon. Instructor Kemp, a young woman with a petite build, yet a very loud voice, had very cold gray eyes that seemed to stare right through you. Yet she was very informative in her part of the training. She took whatever time was necessary with each of us in order to help us pass the firing range with at least a 72 percent mark, even if she had to help us on her own time. Our final instructor was a man named Mr. Cole. He was our favorite of all the instructors because he had a funny way about him. A tall, slender man with dancing green eyes that always seemed to be laughing when he spoke; Mr. Cole would try to make light of our mistakes without forgetting the importance of safety and accuracy.

The day that we went to the firing range for the first time was the scariest for me. I was one of the officers who had never fired a gun before. My hands were shaking so badly that I kept dropping the bullets before I could get my revolver loaded. Finally, Mr. Cole loaded my weapon for me and told me to get a grip and get over my fear of the weapon, or I would never be able to shoot it safely and accurately. By the time I left the firing range, Mr. Cole told me that I was doing "real good." That didn't change the fact that I was scared stiff every time I had to pick up my gun during the training and afterward.

The thing I remembered the most was the last day of training. We had to take our final written test as well as qualify with our weapons. I was so afraid that I would mess up. It didn't help that I was so nervous that Mr. Cole had to talk me through each step before I could even get into the firing booth. When I finally stepped into the booth, the kick from the shotgun was so powerful that Mr. Cole had to stand behind me and hold his hand against my back to keep me from flying out of the booth. It was really kind of humorous, though. By the time I had completed the qualification requirements, I had a very sore shoulder, hand, and back. However, I did pass with a total of 90 percent for my classroom work and 82 percent for the firing range. My fear of handling a weapon had finally subsided, but it was not completely gone.

Stress management was taught by Captain Daniels, whose dark hair streaked with gray showed an air of experience. Yet his brown eyes seemed to be so distant. Captain Daniels taught us how to deal with the everyday stress of being in law enforcement. His main objective was for us to be able to cope with our professional lives while making sure that our personal and family lives didn't fall apart. The course lasted for three days, during which we listened to lectures, watched a couple of short movies, had class discussions, and then took a written quiz at the end of each class. The course was actually a for-your-information class. Everyone passed with flying colors as long as they showed up every day and participated in the class discussions.

Riot control was taught by Lieutenant Majors, a slender man with brown hair and smiling green eyes. He was very serious in his teachings, yet he had a very humane element about him.

The course consisted of three written tests, reading assignments, lectures, and participating in a mock riot. All the riot equipment was kept in the security office of each division. The mock riot involved fifty inmates and twenty-five officers. The inmates started fighting about gang territory in the jail. The two gangs were the Gangster Disciples and the Latin Kings. A group of the Disciples had a bunch of homemade knives called shanks that they were waving in the Latin Kings gang member's faces. Of course then, the Kings got out their shanks to defend themselves. Lieutenant Majors told us that he wanted us to work together to figure out a way to take control of the inmates as well as get all the weapons away from them without anybody getting hurt.

Our plan was to get as many officers into riot gear as possible. Riot gear consists of protective pads for the head, torso area, knees, and arms. We were supposed to take a riot baton with us to the dorm that was rioting. Once we reached the dorm, all the officers stormed the inmates until we had them under control, off the dorm, and all the weapons confiscated. There were a couple of inmates who got hurt as well as three of our officers. None of the inmates or officers were seriously injured or needed to be hospitalized

The US jail standards course was taught by Sergeant Tobin, a short, stocky man in his early thirties who had dancing green eyes that highlighted his wavy blond hair.

The course was meant to educate us about the proper procedures of the jail as well as the rules and regulations that inmates had to follow. The main rule officers had to remember is: only the superintendent of each division can authorize the use of riot gear. The function of all the officers was to prevent escape, prevent contraband (drugs, alcohol, weapons, etc.) from being brought into the jail, prevent inmates from being hurt, supervise inmate movement, make sure all inmates get proper medical attention, receive their mail each day, and get at least one fifteen-minute phone call each week.

During one of Sergeant Tobin's lectures, he expressed how important it was for all of us to stay alert at all times. That way, no inmate could ever leave the dorm or escape. One incident he told us about took place in Division Six when an inmate found a way to unlock one of the exit doors leading to the yard outside the dorm. When he saw that the officer on his dorm wasn't paying attention to the inmates, he rigged the lock on his cell door so that it wouldn't stay locked when Officer Fipps locked the cells for the night. At approximately three o'clock in the morning, the inmate, Sean, looked out of his cell and noticed that Officer Fipps had fallen asleep. Knowing that he wouldn't be caught, he seized the opportunity to escape. Not only did Sean successfully leave his assigned dorm, he also managed to get past the guard in the tower located in the middle of the yard, which was located just before a fence he had to climb over in order to leave the jail ground.

It was almost seven o'clock in the morning when Officer Fipps noticed an inmate was missing. Wiping the sleep out of his sullen blue eyes, he realized he had no option open to him but to contact his immediate supervisor and let him know one of the inmates from his dorm had escaped.

The next step, when an inmate escapes, was to secure the area and contact the chief security department so that they can contact the Chicago Police Department, the director of the jail, and the sheriff.

An investigation was performed, and then a written report had to be turned over to the director of the jail before the officer on-duty during the escape could go home. As a result of the negligence on the part of Officer Fipps, his supervisor wrote him up for inattention to duty. This resulted in him getting a twenty-nine-day suspension without pay. Officer Fipps had to appear in front of the Cook County Merit and Hearing Board for a hearing to present any evidence he might have that would prove he hadn't been negligent in his duties at the time the inmate had escaped. Unfortunately, Officer Fipps ended up getting terminated even though he had been with the county for eight years and was charged with aiding in the escape of an inmate. Although the charges were later dropped, he was never able to work in law enforcement again. What a price to pay for sleeping on the job!

Staying alert at all times, while on the job, was the most important as well as competent way to perform your duties as a Cook County Deputy Sheriff or correctional officer.

Self-defense was the hardest course at the academy. We had three instructors. The first, Officer Penrose, was a short, dark-skinned woman with a nasty disposition. Officer Gale, a tall, thin woman with dark skin and graying hair, had been in the military for many years. This gave her an edge over the other instructors because she was in great physical condition. Finally, there was Officer Fontane. He was of medium height and build with light blond hair and blue eyes that always seemed to be frowning at everyone.

Officer Fontane believed in teaching by punishment methods if you made a mistake. He wouldn't talk to you about what you did wrong; he would make you drop and give him fifty push-ups. If you couldn't do all fifty, or you refused to, he would push you and try to provoke you into hitting him. I remember one time when I didn't hold the riot baton the correct way, Officer Fontane hit me in the head with the baton and told me the next time I messed up, he would kick my ass. Not exactly what I would call professional behavior from an instructor. My response wasn't exactly professional either. I told him to keep his fucking hands off me, or I would stuff the baton up his ass sideways!

Officer Gale was our favorite instructor in self-defense. She would always work with us through everything she wanted us to do. She would use her military knowledge to help us do things properly, and if we didn't, she told us we had to do twenty-five push-ups as a group. Everyone must count together and fall out of place from everyone else. But she still gave us the most encouragement of anyone. When we had to qualify in the mile-and-a-half run in under thirteen minutes, Officer Gale would run with us. She would watch to see which of us had a problem keeping up with the others and would get all those people together before the next time we were supposed to run and then run with them. In most cases, they would make better time running the next time out. There were still a few who never quite made the run in the allotted time. They gave it their best shot though.

Officer Penrose taught us the different techniques we needed to know in order to protect ourselves in case we ever had to make an arrest on the streets. The one part of the training that stood out in my mind was when she taught us the proper way to fall and roll in order to keep from getting seriously hurt. She told us the most important thing to remember: never stand in the open, giving your assailant an unobstructed target to shoot at. Whenever we hear a loud popping noise, we should always assume it was gunfire and look for cover quickly. You should always drop down low, in a crouched position, and then roll out of the direct line of fire.

We had a mock shooting and arrest as part of our training. We got into groups and assigned two people to be the assailants and three people to be the officers. The assailants had just robbed a bank, and both of them had guns.

The call came in about the robbery, and we had to respond immediately.

When we arrived at the bank, the two suspects were just exiting the building with their guns drawn. Dropping down behind our car, we announced that we were deputy sheriffs from the Cook County Sheriffs Department and told them to drop their guns and put their hands in the air. The two suspects started firing at us, leaving us no alternative but to fire back.

I was scared stiff; what should I do? This was the first time I had ever been faced with this type of situation. My next thought was to try to think logically about how to get the situation under control. I looked to my partners for some sort of answer to this problem, and what we came up with was to try to surround the two suspects and force them to surrender. We finally got them to surrender, but not until one of our officers was shot.

Luckily for our officer, it was only a flesh wound, and he was treated at one of the outpatient care centers and then released within a couple of hours.

The two assailants were arrested and charged with robbery and attempted murder of a police officer. They were both found guilty in court and sentenced to eight years in the state penitentiary in Joliet, Illinois.

The many benefits of the self-defense course helped me immensely on the road to becoming a good officer. One thing I always try to remember is: be observant as well as cautious when performing your duties.

By the end of the training academy, I felt pretty confident that I would be a good officer. All the instructors gave us evaluations on our abilities to follow directions, make decisions on our own, and accept criticism without getting angry as well as the importance of being dressed properly for duty each and every day.

My evaluation was excellent across the board; the instructors said that I would make a very good officer, and that they would be proud to work with me.

CHAPTER 5

Psych Training

When I got out of the training academy, I was assigned to Division Eight, a psychiatric ward for inmates with severe mental problems and depression disorders.

Approximately two months after I got out of the academy, I was sent to a four-week psychiatric-training class to help me become more aware of the problems I would be dealing with as well as give me more insight into how to deal with the many different personality disorders I would have to be around. During the training, we all had to visit different mental institutions and talk with patients and conduct interviews at each facility. We then had to write an evaluation as well as give a diagnosis and method of treatment for the patient.

The last part of the training involved watching three different movies on mental disorders and then participating in a discussion after each movie. The movies we viewed were *One Flew Over the Cuckoo's Nest*, *Into Madness*, and *Schizophrenia*. All three movies had to do with the main types of mental disorders: schizophrenia, mental depression, and dysfunctional behavior patterns.

The movies were very informative, *One Flew Over the Cuckoo's Nest* being the best of the three. Jack Nicholson played one of the main characters, John, an inmate in a mental hospital. John had been convicted of a crime that would have given him many years in jail. He chose to go into a mental hospital to avoid doing time in the state penitentiary. All John wanted to do was beat the system and, in doing so, make some of the other patients start to live again instead of just existing. Unfortunately for him, the staff wanted the patients to be constantly drugged and sedated as they were easier to handle that way. One of the nurses decided that John should be overly medicated so he wouldn't cause any problems or buck the system. When that didn't work, they eventually performed a lobotomy on him. That bothered me a lot because all John could do after that was lie in his bed and stare off into space making unintelligible noises and drooling on himself.

The movie *Into Madness* had to do with schizophrenia and mental disorders. There were three people who talked about their illnesses and tried to explain what it was like to have those type of illnesses.

The first patient's name was Sally. She was twenty-four years old and had been diagnosed with schizophrenia at the age of nineteen. She would twirl her fingers through her light-brown hair, chain-smoke, and drink cup after cup of coffee. Sally was in a therapy center for people with the same illness as her own. (They were allowed to go home once a month, for the weekend, to see their families.) Sally would pace the floor in her room or the yard of the hospital in the recreation area talking to herself about things that made no sense at all. One of the things she would say over and over was, "I find it hard to talk to anyone for a long time because everyone says I'm schizophrenic. Maybe I am. Then again, maybe I'm not. Yes, we are." I couldn't imagine having all my thoughts jumbled in my mind all the time. That would be very frustrating for me and others as well.

The second patient whose story was told was a young man named Charles. He was only twenty years old and was in the habit of staring off into nowhere, making his hazel eyes seem distant as he fingered his dark-brown hair. There was a history of mental disorders in the last two generations of his family. Charles had spent most of his life in institutions. All he really wanted out of life was to be able to live on his own and think clearly. Nothing in his life ever came easily; school especially was difficult because he couldn't concentrate with all the mental turmoil going on inside his head. The main thought Charles sent out to me was that he never had a normal childhood. His mother was killed in a car accident when he was only three years old, and his father was a hardworking construction worker who never came to see Charles because he couldn't deal with his son's illness.

The third patient was an eighteen-year-old girl named Paula. Paula constantly pulled at her red hair and stared aimlessly into space with clear blue eyes that always had a crystal shine to them from her medication. Barely eighteen, she had spent a good part of her life in institutions; the first when she was only fifteen years old. After several months of incoherent and nonsensical rambling, Paula's mother decided it would be best if she was institutionalized for observation. Paula was diagnosed as schizophrenic with mental depressive episodes that could only be controlled by medication. While Paula was there, she tried to kill herself twice. The first time she used a bedsheet and tried to hang herself. The second time she stored up her medication and took an overdose. Luckily, at both times, someone found her before it was too late. She heard a voice telling her to do it, so she did. Because she never fully recovered, she had stayed in institutions ever since.

I wish I could have done something to help those patients to recover or at least get better, especially Charles as he was the one who had the roughest life for such a young guy.

When we visited the mental facilities, I interviewed a patient named Gordon. He was very withdrawn, sullen and appeared to be in his own little world. Gordon was in his late twenties and stood about six feet tall. He would brush back his dark curly hair whenever he spoke. He told me that he didn't want to live anymore because nobody cared if he lived or died. I asked Gordon why he felt that way. He responded in a low, sad voice saying, "My family locked me up several times when I was a young boy." As he looked down with his sad green eyes, he stated, "They have always told me that I am nothing but trouble to them."

I felt really bad for Gordon, as he appeared to have given up on life. I tried to be understanding and gentle with him while I performed my interview so that he would feel at ease. During the interview, he told me about his childhood: how his father was an alcoholic and would beat him every time he got drunk. That told me that he was a very troubled and introverted person. Gordon didn't really know how to express love or happiness, only anger and sadness.

The interview lasted approximately thirty minutes. Then Gordon started getting edgy and irritable, so I felt it was best to cut the interview short so I wouldn't upset him further. My diagnosis of him was that he was suffering from a severe case of dysfunctional mental disorder, and I would have him go through some intense therapy as well as take a mild antidepressant. Hopefully, in time, he will feel better about himself and then maybe be able to live a normal healthy life outside mental institutions. The instructor told me that my diagnosis and course of treatment were both correct for Gordon.

CHAPTER 6

Promotion or Scam

I was with the county a little over a year when I decided to take the sergeants' promotional exam. What a joke that was. After spending more than a month studying for the exam, I took it for the first time in June of 1991. The exam took almost five hours from start to finish.

The first part of the exam contained 150 questions about US jail standards. The next part had a hundred questions on the procedures of the different jobs. The last part had seventy-five questions about the different responsibilities and methods of handling situations as a sergeant in the different divisions.

The exam was made up of true/false, multiple choice, short answer and opinion questions. The majority were multiple choice. We all called it the multiple-guess section.

The questions on the exam dealt with things such as size regulation of the cells at the jail, type of meals, including calorie intake, the inmates were supposed to receive, how many hot meals per day, and what beverages they were supposed to be given at each meal. It also dealt with questions of how often they were allowed to make phone calls, how much time should be allotted per call, how often per week they were supposed to get recreation, either inside or outside, what medical treatment they were entitled to, and how many showers, sinks, toilets, and drinking fountains, according to law, there were supposed to be for the inmates on each dorm.

The next category of questions had to do with the nature of the crimes committed by individual inmates. The division wherein the inmate was to be housed was based entirely on the type of crime. Murder, rape, assault, molestation, and major drug cases were housed in Division One. Self-defense, minor drug cases, driving under the influence of alcohol, theft, burglary and assault without a weapon were housed in Division Five. Traffic violations, nonpayment of child support, drunk and disorderly conduct, lewd behavior, and unpaid parking tickets were housed in Division Seven. Domestic violence, stalking, and simple robbery were housed in Division Two. All females were housed in Division Four. All mentally impaired males were housed in the RTU (Recovering Treatment Unit) building of Division Eight. Females were housed in the ACU (Acute Care Unit) section of Division Four. All male inmates with drug or alcohol addictions were housed in the drug unit of Division Eight. All other inmates were housed in divisions Nine, Ten, and Eleven. Age and sex were also taken into consideration when housing inmates as well as whether or not they had any medical problems or mental impairments. The last factor in housing inmates was the amount of their bond. Some had no bond at all because of the severity of their crimes.

Finally, there were questions having to do with the responsibilities, procedures, and proper methods of handling situations as a sergeant in each division. Things such as assigning responsibility for notifying the captain of the division when there was a fight or a major incident. Does the sergeant do it or the lieutenant? Who would be the one in charge of calling an "all available" when a riot breaks out in a division? The correct answer was the shift commander. If a fire breaks out or any other natural disaster, who was responsible for calling the proper departments for help? The division's superintendent or a designated shift commander was the correct response.

Once the test was over, we had to wait almost three months just to get the results. Then there was another three-month wait before we received our certification letters along with the date and time for our interview. After we had our interview, we had to wait another six months to a year and a half to find out if we got the promotion.

I was on the certification list, and I was one of the first officers interviewed. I was on the promotion list for two years before we were informed that the list had expired and that we had to take the test all over again.

The majority of the officers who were promoted were either males, Afro-Americans, Hispanics, or were individuals who had political affiliations.

After being passed over three times during the two year waiting period of the list, I wrote a letter to the sheriff of Cook County. That ended up going unnoticed and unacknowledged. When the letter didn't get me anywhere, I decided to go to our union. What a mistake that was! I was told that I didn't have enough time in, as an officer, to even be worried about getting a promotion. Still, I knew that many other officers had been promoted who had the same amount of time in as I had as well as some with less time. I truly believed that the key to getting any promotion was strictly political. But just to give it the benefit of a doubt, I took the exam again. Seeing as I had now been with the county for four years, I figured things would be different.

I went through the whole process again. Unfortunately, it didn't make a damn bit of difference. I still got passed over for the promotion again, and I was told it was for the same reasons as the first time. The second time around, I didn't even try to ask anyone any questions about why I was passed over again. I figured why bother. The answers would have been the same. All the reasons were a bunch of bullshit—plain and simple!

CHAPTER 7

Controversy

I was with the Cook County Sheriffs Department for about a year when all the bullshit started. If it wasn't the other officers giving me grief and harassing me, it was the inmates causing me problems. The officers started in with me right after the first sergeants' certification list came out. My name was on the list with five other officers from Division Eight. A lot of the officers who didn't make the certification list were probably just jealous, but that was no excuse to be mean and cruel to someone.

A couple of officers started putting nasty sayings and drawings of me on the walls of the washrooms and locker rooms in the different buildings of Division Eight. It made me feel really bad. I was embarrassed to see and hear the things that other officers had to say about me. The thing that bothered me the most was a crude drawing of me giving a blow job to one of the male officers. Of course, the saying that went with it was, "If she can't get the promotion on her own merit, she'll do whatever she has to do to get it." Then there was the drawing of me stooped over, looking like I was kissing the captain's ass. The caption that went with that drawing was, "I guess it's not so bad being a brownnoser; the captain really likes that in an officer." Finally, there was a drawing of me with my husband. He was squatting down with me sitting on his head. That caption read, "Boy, is this what I look like with hair? I've been bald for so long, I forgot what it was like to have a head of hair."

Besides the harassment of the drawings, there were also phone calls made to the dorms I worked on. When I'd answer the phone, the person on the other end would either hang up without saying a word or would make an obscene comment to me like, "Suck my dick, bitch," and then they would hang up. This would sometimes go on for the entire shift.

Some officers would just blurt out things in roll call to me like "Did you send your check downtown yet? To pay for your promotion? When are you going to call on your political clout? Oh, that's right, supposedly you don't have any clout." Another of their favorite things to say was, "How long did you have to stay on your knees in order to pass the exam?" It wouldn't have been so bad except for the fact that many of the other officers would laugh at what was being said. Then some of them would add their own comments, whereas, most of the time, those officers wouldn't say anything to me.

Next to join in the harassment were the brass members in the division. I really didn't expect them to get involved in it as they were supposed to set a good example for the officers.

There was this one sergeant, his name was Fagrina, and what a bastard he was. Every chance he got, he would criticize me, call me names, and tell me how he was going to fuck with me for as long as I worked in the same division as him. He would give me really bad assignments and talk shit about me to the inmates. Sergeant Fagrina would always push his thin blond hair off his face with his thick fingers as he spoke. The fact that we were supposed to stick together, where dealing with the inmates was concerned, seemed to be lost on Sergeant Fagrina, who often talked about me to them. That just made my job that much more hectic and difficult to perform.

Then the inmates started in with their comments and refusing to do what I would tell them to do because of all the shit they had heard about me from the sergeant.

One incident that really stood out in my mind was when this inmate named Fernando called me a "fucking bitch" and said that he'd heard I was willing to do anything to get what I wanted. He then stated, with fire in his green eyes, that he would like to have a piece of me himself. That was very embarrassing to me, and it pissed me off. My only recourse was to write him up and to have him put in an isolation cell for a couple of hours.

Another incident that was very irritating to me was when an inmate named Dehlmer, a heavyset man with broad shoulders, came up to me one day while I was working his dorm and told me he was going to rape me and then beat the shit out of me. As he pushed back his dark-brown hair, he said, "No one will care, either, because you're nothing but a slut according to the officers here." That really scared me because of the way he looked at me with those spooky green eyes of his.

When the officers got wind of what had happened, it triggered more rumors and more harassment. I told my supervisor what had happened with the officers, and nothing was done about it.

All that happened was that the brass started giving me more grief and told me that there was nothing they could do about it, so I should just ignore it and do my job. That pretty much was the county's way of dealing with any situation involving an officer who was not liked: just bury the problem under a rug or conveniently lose the paperwork before it can be sent to the investigations department. If it was not acknowledged, then they don't have to do anything about it. How convenient for them.

I lived through a lot of grief, harassment, personal assaults, and verbal assaults from many different levels during the five years I was with the county. It didn't matter how hard I tried to do my job to the best of my ability; someone always gave me a hard time or put me down in order to make themselves look better.

When you draw too much attention to the department you work in, other officers and brass members who were politically affiliated will say and do anything to try to get you fired. One such incident that comes to mind was when I wrote up an inmate named Tyrone for offering me a twenty-dollar bill to bring him cigarettes to the jail. I notified my supervisor of the incident and did everything I was supposed to do according to county rules and regulations. But the next thing I knew, I was called into investigations and accused of accepting a bribe from an inmate. Luckily for me, I was able to prove I had not accepted the bribe from that inmate or any other inmates.

I showed the investigators my written report along with copies of the money and the serial number from the twenty-dollar bill that I had already turned in to my supervisor.

That only solved the one problem, and there were many others that followed. It didn't matter what I did after that; there were periodic allegations of bribery, physical contact with inmates in unprofessional ways, letters and phone calls allegedly made from my inmates to me at home as well as allegations of me dating inmates.

It never ceases to amaze me the things that people will say and do when they were jealous of someone. Some will go as far as to cost another person his or her job.

Working for the Cook County Department of Corrections has got to be one of the most mind-taxing jobs I've ever had. All I ever wanted was to have a well-paying job so my family and I could live a comfortable life.

CHAPTER 8

Riots

Even the quiet divisions of the jail had riots. The very first riot I remember, while I was working at the county, was in Division Five in 1991. The entire division was on lockdown because a big drug kingpin had escaped a few days before. His name was Kurop. He was from Turkey. He had major connections with gangs as well as drug dealers and was very intelligent when it came to getting what he wanted. According to investigations of the escape, Kurop bribed an officer into helping him to get a brass member's uniform. He then helped to get him to an area from where it would be easy to get off the compound without getting caught, found the perfect time to escape, and had a security car waiting by the dock door of the receiving area of the jail in Division Five.

After the escape, it took the director of the jail about five hours to inform the sheriff and other authorities of the escape. Why was that? Rumor had it that he was in on the escape and wanted to give Kurop enough time to get away. Why else would a security car be used to drive Kurop off the compound and take him directly to the airport? (Kurop was seen at the airport within an hour and a half after he had escaped from the jail.)

The entire jail was put on lockdown approximately three hours after the escape. Division Five was the only division to stay on lockdown for almost a week afterward. In fact, that was exactly what caused the riot that took place.

At approximately 2:20 p.m. in August of 1991, all hell broke loose in Division Five. One dorm after another erupted in fights until the whole division had inmates fighting inmates, officers fighting inmates, and the riot squad trying to break up the fights. The riot was out of control for at least five hours with many inmates and officers injured. Some injuries sustained were bad enough that the wounded had to be taken to an outside hospital. There were ambulances lined up all the way out to the street in front of the jail for hours, waiting to load up officers and inmates who needed to get to the hospital immediately. There were a couple of officers who had severe facial and head injuries as a result of the rioting. Those not so badly hurt were treated at Cermak Hospital at the jail.

The next riot that took place at the jail was approximately two months later. This one was in Division One on the second floor of the dorms in the older area of the division. Three dorms erupted, one right after the other. Many officers, as well as inmates, were hurt but not as badly as in the last riot. One of the officers was stabbed in the neck and needed to get stitches right away. Luckily for him, it wasn't a deep cut. He was able to return to work a week later. There were two inmates who were hurt severely; both of them needed to be taken to the hospital. They were lucky. They were both released from the hospital about a week later. The entire incident was over within an hour, which was really unusual for a riot. The officers and brass members involved were very professional and reacted quickly.

Two inmates from rival gangs started the riot. One was from the Black Gangster Disciples, and the other one was from the Latin Kings. Both gangs got involved to help individual members of their gangs. The initial cause of the riot was gang members fighting over territorial rights in their divisions. They both wanted to be the shot-callers for the dorm, but there can only be one gang running everything in a particular area. After weeks of verbal confrontations between the two gang members, they finally met to see if they could somehow reach an agreement. Unfortunately, they couldn't, and when all else failed, they decided to take action by fighting among themselves. Shanks (homemade knives) were the weapons they used to stab and cut each other with. (Inmates had plenty of time to make them each day of their incarceration.)

Officers had riot batons and cushioned riot gear to protect themselves. There were inmates who picked up chairs, mops, mop wringers, and tables to use as weapons as well as using their shanks. As a result of the riot and the damages caused by it, all the inmates in Division One were put on lockdown for one week.

Any time there was a major fight or riot in any division, they were automatically put on lockdown for at least twenty-four hours following the disturbance. All inmates involved in the riot, as well as the officers involved, were supposed to be checked out thoroughly by medical staff and then sent to the hospital if they need any further medical attention.

There was a riot in Division Ten around the middle of October of 1992, when several inmates got a hold of shanks and used them on a couple of officers. What started the fight was Officer Gant telling his inmates to go to their cells for the 9:00 p.m. count and one inmate refusing to do it. Officer Gant called for Officer Rudy, who was working across the hall, to back him up so he could get the inmate in his cell. Before Officer Rudy could get there, two inmates jumped Officer Gant and had him on the ground. Officer Rudy tried to get the inmates off Officer Gant, but the two inmates turned on him and beat the shit out of him.

Approximately six months after the riot in Division Ten, there was another riot in Division One. This time, there were several dorms that went up at the same time. This particular riot was started because of two gang chiefs from rival gangs being locked up in ABO, a round-the-clock security area for inmates convicted of major crimes. Inmates were only allowed out of their cells for one hour per day to shower and make a phone call. The rest of the gang members were pissed off at the fact that their chiefs were threatening to kill each other.

When the riot kicked off, the two chiefs, having just been out of their cells for an hour, had been returned to their cells about ten minutes before. Of the inmates and officers involved, about fifteen inmates were hurt pretty badly, but only five of the officers were hurt as bad. There were several other officers and inmates who needed minor medical attention. Within a couple of hours, everything was back under control, and all inmates from the division were on lockdown. They were told they would stay on lockdown for at least seventy-two hours. The supervisors—in the area where the two chiefs were locked up—informed the inmates that they would not be allowed to make any phone calls for the next three days. They could not be out of their cells at the same time either.

When the riot in Division Nine happened, it was an unexpected one as the division had only been open about six months. The supervisors were still trying to get everything in order with the inmates' movements. One night, just before lockup, several inmates on various dorms decided that they weren't going to go to their cells. The officers working the dorms called for backup to try to get the inmates in their cells, but all of them called at the same time. Some of the officers couldn't get anyone to back them up when they needed it, and their inmates got out of control. Tables, chairs, and mop wringers were thrown around the dorms; inmates used their fists to fight with the officers and other inmates who tried to help the officers.

The supervisors in charge that night had to go to each and every dorm where there were problems. That was the proper procedure followed by the county whenever there was any kind of a disturbance on the dorms in their divisions. When the inmates refuse to lock up, it always presents a problem because then you had to try to lock up the inmates who were willing to be locked up and keep your eye on the inmates who aren't. By the time officers finally got around to all the dorms to lock all the inmates up, there were several inmates as well as officers who had gotten hurt.

No inmates or officers had to be hospitalized, although some had to be sent to the emergency room at the jail to be checked out and bandaged.

Once everything was taken care of, and all the inmates were locked up for the night, the supervisors had to write the reports and make sure the superintendents of their divisions were notified. That took them each an additional hour to do.

CHAPTER 9

Director or Executioner

The director of the Cook County Jail was a man named B. S. Fairlane. He was a tall, dark-skinned man with salt and pepper hair and mean-looking brown eyes. Fairlane always has his bodyguards around him because he doesn't like officers to approach him. Ever since Fairlane joined the staff at the county jail in December of 1990, there has been one problem after another.

The safety of the officers has never been his number one concern. It didn't matter to him if the officers were attacked by inmates or injured by unsafe working conditions just as long as they showed up for work.

There had been at least three escapes, half a dozen riots, and several officers had been injured severely enough to be off from work for weeks or months. As well, there had been many lawsuits filed against both Fairlane and the county by officers and inmates all in just the four years of his being the director.

I remember the first time I met Fairlane. It was in the elevator in Division Five. I was dressed in civilian clothes and on my way to the personnel office to pick up my paycheck. He said hello to me, and we talked briefly on the way upstairs.

The next time I saw him, I was in full uniform on my way into the jail to go to work. He looked at me as if I were a piece of shit on the ground when I tried to talk to him. All he said to me was that he doesn't talk to officers. His bodyguards quickly stepped between

Fairlane and myself and told me that the director didn't have time to be bothered and to get on my way.

Whenever there was a fight, a riot or any type of disturbance at the jail, Fairlane would blame the officers, saying that we weren't doing our jobs properly. He took every opportunity he could to make the officers look bad.

One incident that stood out in my mind was the time Kurop escaped from Division Five. First of all, Kurop was in jail for a major crime and should have been housed in Division One under constant watch and not in a minimum security area of the jail in a worker's position. All inmate workers had complete movement within their division as well as when they were taken to other divisions to perform their daily duties. Even though they were escorted by officers to all areas of the jail, the inmates can still get into trouble as well as do things that they couldn't do if they were confined to their division only: things like trading drugs, money, or street clothes to other inmates in exchange for favors. No inmate convicted of a violent crime or a crime in a major category was supposed to be a worker, so why was Kurop allowed to be a worker? Why wasn't he housed properly? Why did the director wait several hours after Kurop escaped to report it? Could it be that the director was in on it from the very beginning? Rumor had it Fairlane was on the take when Kurop escaped. Anything was possible, especially at the county.

There were quite a few incidents at the jail during Fairlane's administration that never happened during the directorship of others. Why were they happening then? Was it coincidence or just bad politics?

As the director, Fairlane was only concerned with his own well-being and that of a few select people who worked for him in upper-management positions.

When the riot took place in Division Five, about a week after Kurop had escaped, the director blamed the officers for the riot. One of his spokespersons told the press that he had ordered the officers to take the inmates off lockdown, and that we refused to do it. What a crock of shit that statement was!

What really happened was that the director had given a direct order throughout Division Five that all inmates were to remain on lockdown until he gave the officers other instructions. On the day of the riot, before Fairlane left for the day, he hadn't said anything about letting the inmates off lockdown at any time that evening. In fact, during the evening shift's roll call, there was an announcement made that Division Five was still under lockdown and would remain that way until further notice from the director. Fifteen minutes into the shift, the announcement came to all divisions that there was a riot in Division Five, and they needed all available officers to assist.

Several officers from Division Eight, the division I worked in as well as other divisions went over to Division Five to get the riot under control. This left divisions all over the jail short of officers for the duration of the riot. Safety throughout the jail was jeopardized for several hours that night. Why wasn't outside help from the Chicago Police Department called in to lend a hand?

According to the director, we didn't need any extra help at the jail that night because it was only a minor disturbance. Not many inmates or officers were hurt, and no one was severely injured. He was a fucking hypocrite; there were a lot of severe injuries.

What really happened as a result of the riot was never told to the press. Not even when the director and the sheriff were questioned about it at a later date. There were at least thirty officers and over one hundred inmates hurt during the riot. There were seventeen officers taken to Cook County Hospital, and close to one hundred inmates taken there as well.

Whenever there has been an incident at the jail, Fairlane has always played it down, blamed the officers for not doing right, and told the spokesperson of the jail to tell only half-truths. He will do anything to make himself look good and his officers look incompetent. Officers were not allowed to talk to the press or give any kind of statement regarding anything that goes on in the jail. So none of us could tell the press what had really happened that night. Could it be that Fairlane didn't want the news media to know what really goes on in the jail? I believe that was exactly it, because he would then have to admit he made mistakes.

During the five years I worked for the county, there had been a handful of officers and brass members who had anonymously spoken to the newspapers and news stations on television. All they wanted to do was let the public knew what really went on at the jail.

Somehow, the director and the sheriff always came out on top. Why was that? It had a lot to do with who they gave their interviews to, what contributions were given by what people, and what information they chose to include when speaking to reporters and interviewers.

I remembered seeing Fairlane, along with the sheriff, on the news one night after a riot at the jail. They both described it as a minor disturbance. They lied through their teeth; it was far from a minor disturbance. Director Fairlane referred to the officers as jail guards and stated that we had not done our jobs, saying that if we had, there never would have been the disturbance at the jail. He couldn't have been more wrong; the officers did everything possible to prevent the riot.

Why was it that every time things go wrong at the jail, the officers were blamed? Could it be because Fairlane refused to take responsibility for anything that went wrong as a result of following his orders? Officers can't always be wrong, can they? Maybe it was not that they were in the wrong, as much as it was that the director won't admit when he was wrong.

I remembered having a meeting with the director, a few of the people from his office, brass members, one of his bodyguards, and several officers in Division Eight's drug unit conference room. The purpose of the meeting was so that the officers could ask the director questions regarding the policies at the jail, the upcoming five-and-two work schedule, parking areas for the officers, and the conditions we were forced to work under.

It didn't matter what questions we asked, his responses were always sarcastic. He was negative to the person asking the question, even vulgar at some points, never answering to the satisfaction of the person asking.

One question in particular that I asked was, "Why aren't the officers allowed to defend themselves against the inmates?" His response was that no officer who worked for him would ever hit an inmate and get away with it as long as he was the director at the Cook County Jail.

Another question was why were we being forced to go on a five-and-two work schedule when we had been working a four-and-two work schedule for years? There was already an attendance problem at the jail. Didn't the director realize that adding another day to the work week would just make things worse for the officers? Did he even care? Obviously, he didn't. His answer to that question was, "I don't care what you want. I am putting everyone on a five-and-two work schedule as soon as I can work out the details."

In conjunction with that question, came the question about what was going to be done about the parking situation after the five-and-two schedule went into effect. His response was that it wasn't his problem. He had his parking spot. The officers' parking lot had nothing to do with him, and it was our problem. None of the officers were very happy with his answer. We still faced the day-to-day problems of where we were going to park our cars when we came to work.

At one point during the meeting, the director swore at one of the officers, telling him that he was a "stupid fucker." Totally unnecessary behavior, not to mention, very unprofessional! The officer was embarrassed and said that he didn't appreciate the way he was being talked to. The director's reply was that he didn't give a shit how the officer felt.

Many of the officers who attended the meeting were afraid that if they spoke out they would pay the consequences later by either being fired or given bad work assignments. Most of them listened and didn't say anything.

And Fairlane played things to his own advantage, making sure that he couldn't be linked to any of the things that happened to or with any of the officers. Pretty convenient for him!

By the end of the meeting, there were quite a few officers who were pissed off and felt the meeting was a waste of time. That was the only open meeting I can remember during my time with the county. There had been many closed meetings before that one and there would be many more after. We heard about those in the form of memos that were read to us at roll call.

Since the five-and-two work week went into effect, the director had changed the sick days allowed per month to less than one day; and only six people, instead of seven, can be off on any one day. Now, you must give seventy-two-hour notice for any day you request off, and you can no longer ask for an emergency-vacation time. According to Director Fairlane, the five-and-two work schedule was supposed to be beneficial to the officers. Just one more example of fucking the officers to benefit himself.

CHAPTER 10

High-Profile Inmates

In every jail, there were always high-profile inmates who made the news every day. Mostly, they were inmates who had killed someone famous or robbed a celebrity. Serial killers and rapists, along with celebrities who had committed crimes, also qualified.

I met several of those inmates while I was working at the Cook County Jail in Division Eight. The first one was a man named Wilkinson. He was a small man, very quiet, yet arrogant and rather complex when it came to getting to know him. He was charged with cutting off his wife's legs after an argument with her, stealing an airplane and flying around the sky with her in a suitcase. He said that he cut off her legs because he was in fear of his life after they quarreled and that she bit his thumb. Wilkinson felt that he hadn't done anything wrong. He said that he stole the plane and flew it around for so long in the hope that it would run out of gas and crash and kill him. Wilkinson was found guilty of murdering his wife and was sentenced to life in prison. He can try for an early release after he serves ten years of his sentence.

The next high-profile inmate was David Dowaliby, a medium-built man, who was charged with murdering his stepdaughter and hiding her body in a vacant field near their house in Blue Island, Illinois. David appeared to be totally surprised that he was even a suspect. His brown eyes grew larger than normal as he listened to the police telling him that a witness had seen a car that looked like his own, with a dark-haired man driving it. On September 11, 1988, the day after Jacqueline disappeared, David was asked to take a polygraph test because there was a broken basement window in his house that appeared to have been broken from the inside. He agreed to it and passed it without a flaw in any of his answers. On the day Jacqueline's body was found, with a rope tied around her neck, David was asked to take another polygraph test. This one came back inconclusive. David thought it was because he had a disagreement with the man giving him the polygraph test. David was told to lie and say yes when he was asked if he had killed Jacqueline. He said he couldn't do that because she was his child, and he would never hurt her.

Even though there wasn't any pertinent evidence that proved David was guilty, the district attorney still charged him and his wife, Cynthia, with the murder of their daughter. In November of 1988, two months after Jacqueline's body was found, both parents were taken into custody for the murder of Jacqueline. After their preliminary hearings were held, Cynthia was released for lack of evidence, which was a blessing in disguise as she had recently found out she was pregnant.

While David was at the Cook County Jail awaiting trial, I talked with him on several occasions. He really was a nice guy who was just a victim of circumstance, and all he wanted to do was find out who killed his stepdaughter. He really loved her a lot and this was killing him inside.

In April of 1990 the trial was held based on circumstantial evidence. After only three days of deliberations, David Dowaliby was found guilty of murder in the first degree and also of concealing a homicide. David was sentenced to forty-five years in maximum-security Statesville Prison in Joliet, Illinois. He stayed at the Cook County Jail for another week before he was sent to Joliet.

Months later, David's attorney found out that evidence had been withheld that would have proven his innocence. So in October of 1991, the Court of Appeals overturned the verdict due to lack of evidence in the case against David Dowaliby. David was released from the Statesville penitentiary in October of 1991. At that time, all he wanted to do was go home to his wife and new baby and try to get on with his life.

Cynthia Dowaliby was waiting outside Statesville Prison with open arms for David. She hugged him, and they answered a few questions for the press. David said that he hadn't had a chance to grieve the death of his stepdaughter, and he still wanted to find out who killed Jacqueline and why. Then they left to go home.

Even though David and his wife had gone through a living hell, with David having to spend eighteen months in the Statesville Penitentiary, he wasn't worried about his own loss as much as he wanted to have his stepdaughter back with him and his wife.

Another high-profile inmate was a man named David Greevers, a very large-boned man with green eyes and dark-brown hair. He was charged with murdering his two children by slamming them against a wall because they wouldn't quit crying. David was a very self-pitying person, who moped around the jail feeling sorry for himself because he got caught. Even though David Greevers admitted to killing his two children, he said that he wouldn't have done it if he hadn't been under the influence of drugs at that time. After approximately nine months of going to court for his case, he was found guilty of two counts of first-degree murder in the deaths of his children. The judge sentenced him to the death penalty which was exactly what David wanted.

The next high-profile inmate was a very strange man named Brady. He was charged with the murders of seven prostitutes along with dismembering and eating some of their body parts. Brady was a rather large man with a crazy air about him. He looked older than his thirty plus years because of the drugs he had been using for so long. Brady was in jail for a little over three years since he was tried on each of the seven murders individually. He was found guilty on all the charges and sentenced to life in prison without the chance of parole.

Another high-profile inmate was a young man named Helmot Hoefer who was charged with murdering Mrs. Oldes, a business associate's wife, for money. He allegedly killed her in her home in Glencoe, Illinois. Helmot Hoefer was a young, gay man with a medium build, who stood about six foot two, had blond hair, blue eyes, wore glasses, and was very intelligent.

The star witness, an American man named Tom, moved to Germany shortly after the murder. He gave his deposition before he left, stating that Helmot Hoefer was with him at the time the crime was supposed to have been committed. To Hoefer's dismay, Tom died of AIDS before the case went to trial, so he wasn't much help to Hoefer after all.

The blood DNA didn't match up, the footprints that were found outside a window at the house didn't match either, yet Hoefer was still held at the county jail and then went on trial for the murder of Mrs. Oldes.

Dean Oldes claimed he knew nothing about the murder and that he didn't kill his wife. He believed that Hoefer had killed her. Later though, Dean Oldes changed his story. It was also learned that he had been sending money to Hoefer at the county jail and accepting collect calls from Hoefer as well as going to the jail to visit him.

After months of being incarcerated at the county jail, Hoefer was tried and found innocent of murdering Mrs. Oldes. Hoefer was finally released a month after that.

Dean Oldes was getting a lot of publicity and was fighting the family for his wife's inheritance. He was never cleared of or charged with the murder of his wife.

The last inmate I met was Peter Burton. He was charged with murdering the parents of a man named Dave for a large insurance policy. Peter was a very likable man who was muscular. He had brown hair, blue eyes, and was very intelligent. He admitted to shooting Dave's parents in their home, but he later stated that he was under the influence of drugs and alcohol at the time of the crime. Peter said he really didn't know why he shot them. He really didn't want to, and he probably wouldn't have if he hadn't been under the influence. He swore that under normal circumstances, he couldn't and wouldn't hurt anybody. Peter has already spent twelve months in jail fighting the case. And if he was convicted, he could spend the rest of his life in jail. He will be spending the majority of his adult life in prison as he was only in his late twenties.

CHAPTER 11

Inmate's Living Conditions

All inmates were supposed to have a cell with at least fifty square feet of floor space and an eight-foot-high ceiling. There were also supposed to be no more than two inmates per cell or forty-four inmates in each dorm. The plumbing facilities were to be at least one prison-type toilet (seatless and tankless) per eight inmates, one washbasin per eight inmates—with hot and cold running water—and one shower stall per eight inmates, also with hot and cold running water. Dormitory settings were supposed to have at least thirty-five square feet of floor space in the dayroom area as well as having securely anchored metal tables, chairs, and/or benches to accommodate each detainee or inmate. All inmates housed in a dormitory setting were allotted a rigidly constructed metal bed with a solid or perforated metal bottom securely anchored to the floor and/or wall. All inmates confined to a detention cell were to have proper ventilation with heating or cooling according to the season of the year, and odors should be easily eliminated.

Most of the inmates at the county jail didn't get the things they were entitled to. Many of the cells, as well as the dormitory settings, were overcrowded and, most of the time, didn't have hot running water for their showers. A lot of the inmates had to sleep on the floor because of all the overcrowding in most of the divisions at the county jail. According to the jail standards, no inmate was supposed to sleep on the floor or be housed in an area that was overcrowded.

Dormitory settings, as well as cell settings, were not supposed to have more than forty-four inmates housed in an area.

The jail was fined several times for each day that they didn't comply with the rules governing the housing of inmates. That didn't seem to matter, though, because overcrowding was still a very big problem at the Cook County Jail.

In addition to the living conditions, inmates were also abused by many of the officers throughout the jail. Some inmates were so afraid of being beat up that they try to stay to themselves and not say or do anything during the times abusive officers were on duty.

I'd talked to several inmates during my five years of working at the county about the conditions as well as the treatment of the inmates by the staff members at the jail.

The first inmate who told me of abuse by staff members was a man named Earl. He was a small man with blond hair and green eyes. He said that Officer Dunbler, a large man with big hands, dark hair, and brown eyes, would beat him up every time he worked the dorm Earl was housed on. Earl told me that Dunbler would take him into the hallway, push him up against the wall, and hit him in the head and stomach with a closed fist until he was physically sick.

A couple of times, Earl filed a grievance against the officer, that only resulted in him getting beat up by Officer Dunbler's supervisor, Sergeant Rugby.

Rugby was a chubby, dark-skinned man with dark hair and brown piercing eyes. When Sergeant Rugby confronted Earl about the grievance filed against Officer Dunbler, he told Earl that the grievance would not go any further. He also told Earl to keep his mouth shut about what had happened with the officer, or he would get his ass kicked again, only it would be much worse. Whenever Dunbler worked the dorm, Earl was so scared that he kept quiet about what had happened and stayed as far away from Officer Dunbler as he could.

Another inmate who was abused by the staff was a young guy named Nathan. He was only eighteen years old when he got locked up at the county jail. Nathan was a small, slightly built man with light-brown hair and green eyes. He was very quiet and kept away from the other inmates; he seemed to be an introvert.

The officer who abused him was a rather large man named Gilly. Officer Gilly didn't like Nathan because he was an Afro-American and wouldn't give his food tray or his commissary to inmates who were in the crowd with Officer Gilly. Nathan told Gilly that some inmates on the dorm were taking his food trays and bullying him into giving up his commissary every week. All Nathan got for his troubles was a beating from Officer Gilly and several inmates. They took Nathan into the shower area of the bathroom and took turns hitting him in the face and head with their clenched fists until Nathan passed out. The things which stood out in Nathan's mind were Officer Gilly's big hands and his cold blue eyes.

Jose was another abused inmate. He was about twenty years old, had rich dark hair, sea-green eyes, a medium build, and was gay. Officer Randello beat the shit out of Jose because he was gay, and Randello thought all gays were disgusting. Officer Randello was a large-framed man with huge hands and a very nasty disposition—especially when it came to homosexuals. Officer Randello always badgered Jose when he worked the dorm Jose was housed on. Jose tried to avoid him as he could see the hatred in Randello's eyes whenever he looked at him.

One night, while Officer Randello was working on Jose's dorm, Randello kept yelling at him and calling him a fucking queer. Officer Randello figured if he provoked Jose into hitting him, he could beat the shit out of Jose without getting into trouble. When Jose finally got tired of it, he told Officer Randello that he wanted to see his supervisor. Officer Randello told Jose to shut his fucking mouth and sit the hell down on his bunk.

Jose went to his bunk, but he kept insisting that he wanted to speak to the officer's supervisor. When Officer Randello refused his request for the third time, Jose said that he was going to call his attorney and file a complaint against Randello and the county.

Before Jose could do that, Randello took him into the hallway and beat the shit out of him, giving him a bloody nose, fracturing several of his ribs, and giving him a black eye. After Randello got done, he called medical staff for Jose and told them he had been beaten by another inmate. Jose was so scared that he kept his mouth shut, and the medical staff figured it was like the officer had said.

There were hundreds of inmates who were abused both mentally and physically at the Cook County Jail. Some of them didn't say anything about the unfair treatment they received, and others had filed lawsuits against the officers and the county. Most of the suits filed against the county took years to be settled; while others still hadn't been settled. They may never be settled.

The food that the inmates were served for their meals was supposed to be hot and fresh. If they were lucky, one out of three meals was hot, but usually not fresh. Most of the time, their lunches were sandwiches with spoiled meat and dinners consist of leftovers.

Medical attention for the inmates was at an all-time low. If an inmate asked to see a nurse, he was told to wait until medication was dispensed on his dorm—even if it was not for several hours.

An inmate named Hector was having a seizure one night while I was working on his dorm. I called for the nurse three times before one finally showed up at the dorm, even though, I had told them it was an emergency. Hector was in his late twenties and was a very sickly person because of the seizures as well as the fact that he was an alcoholic. He took medication to control the seizures, but it didn't always control them. Hector died as a result of the medical staff's negligence. His family filed a lawsuit against the county for the wrongful death of their son.

There was an inmate named Baxter who was only twenty-one years old when he was at the Cook County Jail for the first time. One night, while he was housed in Division Nine, there was a fight on his dorm; and Baxter was beaten to death with a mop wringer by an inmate who was twice his size. Baxter wasn't a very large man. He had small hands, a small build, and stood barely five feet tall. On the night he died, he had gotten into a fight with another inmate and the officer working his dorm didn't call for backup right away. He decided to let the inmates fight until one of them got tired or hurt really bad before he would try to break up the fight.

Baxter's parents and his wife filed a lawsuit against the county and the officer for the wrongful death of Baxter. After several years of court hearings, they were finally awarded a large settlement. Although no amount of money could ever take away their pain and sense of loss, it did help them to pay for the funeral as well as give them some money to move away and try to start their lives again.

CHAPTER 12

Working Conditions

The working conditions at the Cook County Jail were below proper standards according to Illinois law. Any unsafe conditions or situations that were detrimental to a person's health should be corrected immediately. Not at the county, though. It was easier to just ignore it. We had been exposed to inmates with active hepatitis, full-blown AIDS, tuberculosis, various venereal diseases, as well as a variety of other minor illnesses.

I remember one time in particular. I was sent to the county hospital to watch an inmate who was really sick. Nobody told me the inmate had full-blown AIDS until later in my shift. When I arrived at the county hospital, the officer who I relieved didn't tell me what was wrong with the man I was going to be watching. He just got the hell out of there as fast as he could. Four hours after I arrived at the hospital, one of the nurses, a woman by the name of Crystal, told me about the inmate's condition. She was a light-skinned Afro-American woman with dark curly hair and a sweet disposition which showed in her sparkling brown eyes.

The inmate's name was Donny. Although he was only twenty-two years old, he looked much older. He had thinning blond hair, sunken blue eyes, and a skinny body due to the extent of the AIDS. I had already looked in on Donny three times in my first couple of hours at the hospital. So if there was any way of getting any viruses from him, I would have already contracted them.

The staff at the county just didn't believe in telling its employees vital information before they actually came in contact with inmates with serious illnesses or diseases. After an outbreak of hepatitis at the jail, the medical staff offered the employees free hepatitis shots. Better late than never!

Over the years, several officers had contracted tuberculosis from inmates at the jail. They weren't even told the inmates had it until after the officers started getting the symptoms.

There were three officers from Division Six who got really sick and developed cancer. Two of those three officers died within months of being diagnosed with the cancer.

One of the officers who died was named Phil Duboise. He really was a nice guy to work with. I worked with him in Division Six for my first year at the county. I met Phil during my first week in Division Six. He was a dark-skinned, Afro-American with dark curly hair, brown eyes, and he had a rather strange sense of humor. Phil would pick on me and tell me that I was a little runt, but that I was his little girl. Phil loved to smoke cigars, which he quit doing when he found out he had cancer. His doctor told him that the cancer was caused by some sort of asbestos at the jail in the division he had been working in for the past several years. I wish he hadn't died because he really was a sensitive person in his own way.

In addition to officers getting very sick and/or dying, many had been injured on the job due to unsafe working conditions. Several officers received broken bones from fighting with the inmates in different divisions. Some had facial and head wounds from getting hit with mop buckets and wringers as well as back injuries from falling on tables and against walls during altercations with inmates or while in the process of trying to break up fights between inmates.

Another major work condition that needs to be corrected was the employee parking lots. There were over two thousand people working at the jail who need to park their cars during their eight-hour shift; there were only five hundred parking spots available. Many officers had gotten tickets for parking their cars on the streets by the jail or have had their vehicles broken into, stolen, or towed as a result of the lack of available parking. Reports had been written regarding the incidents as well as lawsuits filed against the county. Unfortunately, the only thing that happened was that the officers involved were given suspension days for parking their cars in unauthorized areas inside the compound. In the time that I'd been working for the county, I had heard of at least three officers whose cars had been stolen or broken into. My car was vandalized a couple of times too.

If you missed too much work, you got written up and/or suspended without pay for two to twenty-nine days. Some consolation for getting your car stolen or broken into.

There was a female officer who I worked with in Division Eight for a couple of years named Officer Jackson. She had red hair, green eyes, and was a bit on the husky side for being five foot four and only twenty-one years old. After her car was stolen from where she had it parked on the street across from the jail (along with her gun which was in the car), she got written up and was suspended because she didn't have her gun in the armory.

Many officer's guns had been missing or had been damaged when they left them in the armory. This was due to the negligence and dishonesty of those officers working in the armory. Nothing had ever been done to them.

As with any other place of employment, there were good officers as well as bad officers. I'm going to tell you about the good ones first.

Officer Copeland was a short, dark-skinned female with dark hair, brown eyes, and has a very warm air about her. We met in Division Six when I started working at the county. I was only a cadet in training, and she had already been with the county for several years. She was very helpful during my training: showing me how to do the paperwork, deal with the inmates and staff, and perform every part of my job. Everyone called her "Mama C" because she was like a mother to everyone. She was always helping people do their jobs better, and she was never too busy if someone needed her for anything.

Another good officer was Officer Maury. She was a tall, slender, light-skinned Afro-American with red hair, green eyes, and a sweet disposition. I also met her when I was a cadet in Division Six. Seeing as she was just out of the academy and a new officer herself, we hit it off right away. Officer Maury told me a little about the academy and what I'd be doing as well as what to expect from the instructors. I really enjoyed working with her and talking with her. She was always cheery and had time for me whenever I needed or wanted to talk about anything.

When I got out of the academy and went to Division Eight in December of 1991, Officer Maury had already been transferred there. It was really nice to have someone there who I knew and could talk to. She worked in the security office, and I worked on the different dorms in the division. She helped me whenever I had a problem with inmates or officers and when my paperwork got messed up. In the five years I've been with the county, she and I have become really good friends. She was also given the award for the Officer of the Month a couple of times in 1994.

Then there was officer Mackey, another officer who I met in Division Eight. She was a nurse when we first met. About six months after we met, she decided that she wanted to be an officer, so she went through the training. Officer Mackey was a tall, heavyset Afro-American woman. She had green eyes and dark-brown hair. Mackey also had a really terrific sense of humor and was nice to everyone she worked with.

When Officer Mackey got out of the academy, she was assigned to Division Eight, so we worked together on the dorms and in the same areas. Occasionally, we would go out to dinner. From the first time we worked together, we got along really good because we both worked hard and stayed on our assignments like we were supposed to. We never had personality conflicts.

Officer Mackey was one of the few officers who would take up a collection for employees who had a birthday, a baby, or death in the family. Most of the other officers would put money in if they liked the person, but they wouldn't come up with the idea themselves. They just didn't care enough unless it was for them or someone they knew really well.

Officer Hazelwood was another officer I really enjoyed working with in Division Eight. We got along from the start because we both liked to joke around while we worked, and we found it easy to talk to each other. He was a medium-built Afro-American with green eyes, brown curly hair, and a great sense of humor. Officer Hazelwood and I worked together on the same dorms for about six months in the drug unit. Later, we were assigned dorms together in the RTU building for another six months. When we worked together, our dorms ran smoothly, and we backed each other up whenever there was a problem. Neither one of us got hurt by any of the inmates on our dorms, either. Officer Hazelwood would always tease me and tell me that he really liked working with me because I would do my share of the work and then some. He would also tell me that I was funny because I would say and do things to make him laugh, especially when he was down in the dumps.

Officer Palmer was another officer I enjoyed working with. She was a light-skinned Afro-American woman in her early twenties with dark-brown hair and smiling brown eyes. She was very friendly and always seemed to be in a good mood. I met Officer Palmer when she was a cadet in Division Eight and I was an officer. We started talking to each other the first day we met and found we had a lot in common. She always seemed to know when someone was feeling blue or bothered about something, and she would try to make them feel better by talking to them or just listening to what was on their minds. After Officer Palmer got out of the academy, she came back to Division Eight. We talked about the academy when we worked on dorms together in the RTU building and in the drug unit.

Another good officer was Officer Hilley, now a sergeant. She was in Division Eight at the same time I was. She worked a different shift than I did, but we always saw each other at shift change and would talk about work-related and personal things. Officer Hilley was a little older than me; she had reddish hair, brown eyes, and a light complexion for an Afro-American. She was a very sweet lady.

Officer Hilley and I took the sergeants' exam together (the second time I took it) and we both passed. We discussed some of what we thought would be on the test before we took it. She got promoted about eight months after we took the test. I was really happy for her, yet I was a bit upset that I hadn't been promoted as well. I felt I deserved it just as much as she did.

Officer Gluzsek, a Caucasian woman with dark hair and brown eyes, stood about five foot two, and was a little on the chunky side. She was another good officer, who I met while I worked at the jail. She came to Division Eight right out of the academy. I was already there as an officer. I was one of the first people to make her feel welcomed in the division when she first arrived, and we hit it off right away. Officer Gluzsek and I became really good friends almost immediately as we had a lot in common. We were able to talk about anything with each other. We both had teenage sons and had been divorced before. We enjoyed our jobs and worked well together.

Just as every place of employment had good officers, they also had bad officers. The Cook County Jail was no exception.

The first officer I met, who I thought was a bad officer, was a man named Burray. He was in Division Six when I first started working for the county as a cadet in February of 1990. Officer Burray was a very arrogant man. He had dark hair, brown eyes, stood about six feet tall, and had a medium build and dark skin. He was always chasing after the women in the division. He made a pass at me the first time I met him. I told him that I wasn't interested and that I was married, but neither fact seemed to matter to him. All he ever seemed to do while he was working was flirt with the females he came in contact with. I never saw him doing anything but walking around and trying to get women to go out with him. He was married and had at least one child I knew of, yet that didn't seem to be very important to him. I never could trust him as a fellow employee much less as a human being. Officer Burray got into a lot of trouble with the brass in Division Six. I remember he was written up several times for various reasons, ranging from tardiness to insubordination.

Officer Toskin, an Afro-American with a very sick sense of humor, was another bad officer. He would put the make on every female in Division Eight or any other division he worked in or went to during the course of his shift. He would use his dark-brown eyes to his advantage; you could say those were his flirting tools. Officer Toskin was already working in Division Eight when I arrived there.

He was overly friendly from day one, which gave me an eerie feeling about him right away. He never had to work dorms like the other officers did; he was either working the posts, working area, or just hanging around the officers who were assigned to their posts.

I remember one time when I worked on a dorm in the same building, Officer Toskin was working in, and I called for an officer to back me up because of a disturbance on my dorm. Officer Toskin was standing in the hall outside my dorm, so I asked him to come inside and help me. His response was that he wasn't the one I needed to call; I should call the post and have them send someone to my dorm to help. Not a very professional attitude to have, but that was the only one a lot of the officers seem to have, especially after they had been with the county for a few years. Not that it was a good reason to be that way, though.

Then there was Officer Drowers. She was an older woman with dark gray-streaked hair and dark skin and eyes. She had a very mean disposition and was a racist as well. Officer Drowers and I didn't really get along from day one. The first time we worked together was in the drug unit of Division Eight. She would tell me how to do my job and then walk on my dorm and tell the inmates to do different things than what I had previously told them to do. In general, she would cause a lot of problems for me while I was trying to work.

Finally, one time, when we were working together, she started yelling at me and called me a "white-trash whore" in front of the inmates on my dorm. I had already asked her several times to leave my dorm and quit talking disrespectfully to me in front of the inmates. I finally had to put her in her place when she said that I was "white trash" and then called me a "slut" because I had told her that she wasn't being very professional.

After I contacted my supervisor, I wrote a report requesting that she and I not work together anymore. During the conference with her, the supervisor, and myself, she started with the verbal abuse again. I wanted to kick the shit out of her but I didn't.

When the supervisor told her that he was going to write her up for insubordination and unprofessional behavior toward a fellow worker, she got very quiet and admitted she was wrong. I knew that she didn't mean it, and she proved me right as soon as we got back to our assignment. She started in on me again and threatened to cause me more problems than I could handle. My response to her was that she could go fuck herself.

Then there was Officer Bogis. She was the worst officer I ever worked with in Division Eight. She was an Afro-American woman, about five foot seven, and had dark curly hair and brown eyes. She also had a big mouth and made no secret of the fact that she hated white people. We met in the psyche-training class which we all had to attend for four weeks when we were assigned to work in Division Eight. Officer Bogis was very arrogant for a woman. She would come to class late and leave early almost every day. She would talk during class when the instructor was trying to teach, and she felt nobody was as good as she was.

One problem we had was that she would call me on the phone in my dorm and harass me. She would tell me what to do and wouldn't let the inmate workers bring supplies to my dorm when I called the post she was working at. And whenever I wouldn't do what she said, she would call Captain Bully and complain about me.

After being called to the captain's office several times, I finally fought back. I wrote her up for harassment and turned it over to the superintendent of Division Eight. The paperwork got buried, so to speak, and nothing was ever done about it. In fact, I was moved out of the building where she worked. Captain Bully made things really tough on me from that point on.

Another lousy officer was Binton. The first day I met him, I was working in Division Eight in the RTU building. He was a medium-built man with short dark hair and brown eyes. The eyes showed an air of arrogance and a smug confidence that he could get any woman he wanted. When I tried to introduce myself to him, as I did with every officer in the division, he bluntly told me to "shut the fuck up!" He doesn't talk to white women. Talk about being a racist; he never even tried to get to know me as a person or as an officer. Any time he would see me after that, or if he had to relieve me on my dorm when I went to lunch, he would be very rude and belligerent to me.

One time, when he relieved me for lunch, he walked into the dorm to count the inmates; he then came up to the desk to compare his count with the one in the log book. He sat down at the desk without saying a word and started to write in the log book. I got my coat and as I was leaving, I heard him telling the inmates that I was a "bitch" and a "pussy motherfucker." I really didn't appreciate the disrespect or his unprofessional behavior, so I went to my supervisor, very upset by what had just occurred, and talked to him about it.

My supervisor, Sergeant Haney, was very sympathetic, and he rubbed the top of his bald head as he listened. He called Binton to the security office. When he arrived, the three of us discussed what had just happened on my dorm when I was leaving for lunch. When Sergeant Haney asked Officer Binton if he had said the things I had accused him of, he admitted he had. He added that there was nothing Sergeant Haney or I could do about it. When asked why he said those things, his answer was really simple: he said that I was a "bitch," and he didn't like me.

Sergeant Haney told him that wasn't a reason to be rude and unprofessional. Then he told Binton that he should apologize to me. Officer Binton didn't apologize.

Last of all is Officer Krogen. Krogen was about twenty-three years old and a bit on the chubby side. He liked to talk about everybody all the time and to make fun of people. His green eyes had a sneaky air about them as he would say and do cruel things to his fellow workers. He drew some pretty disgusting pictures of my husband and I doing sexual things and wrote nasty graffiti to go along with them and then hung his work up in different areas of the division.

One day an inmate told me that he saw some things written about me in the men's locker room in the RTU building. I asked my husband to go and tell me what was written. He did, and it said, "Officer Wilkinson will blow anyone to borrow money from them." Another drawing had an inmate and me in a compromising position and stated that I would fuck any inmate if I thought I could get something from him. Another drawing Officer Krogen drew was of me holding a carton of cigarettes and a Bible. I was telling an inmate that I would give him the cigarettes for his Bible. Then it said, "If you don't give me your Bible, I'll just take it."

Another reason I feel that Krogen is a bad officer was because he never stayed on the dorms he was assigned to. He always played around instead of doing his job, and he yelled at the inmates, calling them names and beating them just for the hell of it. One night, I remember going to his dorm to relieve him for his lunch break, and he was yelling at an inmate. He then threw the inmate on a bunk and started beating him up. I told Officer Krogen that I felt he was wrong for what he had done. He, in turn, told me to mind my own "fucking business" and to worry about myself.

CHAPTER 13

Drugs in the Jail

Drugs should never be brought into the jail by anybody! Not medical staff, officers, brass members, or visitors. So how was it that drugs get into the jail then? Well, I'll tell you how. Officers, medical staff, brass members, and people who came to visit inmates brought it in.

Nurse Bates brought marijuana in for several inmates in the RTU building of Division Eight once. She had it hidden inside her purse. Obviously, the officers working the security checkpoints weren't doing their jobs properly, or it wouldn't have got past them.

John, one of the inmates who gets diabetic medication, got it from her and brought it back to the dorm for himself and a few other inmates. John was a heavyset man in his late twenties with blond hair and green eyes. He wasn't very bright, though. He went straight to the bathroom when he came back on the dorm. Unfortunately for John, I was the type of officer who thought it was rather suspicious, and I followed him into the washroom and busted him when he took the marijuana cigarettes out of his pants. He was really surprised when I grabbed it out of his hand, ordered him to come with me, and told him he was busted. He tried to talk me out of turning him in, but I told him, "No way." My job was to make sure there wasn't any contraband brought into the jail.

After I notified my supervisor and completed the proper paperwork, John was escorted to the isolation cell. He had to remain there until my supervisor told him he could return to his dorm. The very next day, he was transferred to another medical unit in another division of the jail.

Several officers had been busted over the years for bringing drugs to the inmates as well as accepting money from the inmates' families for bringing the drugs into the jail.

One of the officers was a female named Starlyle. She had only been with the county for about nine months when the urge to make some fast bucks came over her. That turned out to be her downfall. Rumor around the jail was that she was bringing in drugs so the investigations department of the county got involved. What they decided to do was set Officer Starlyle up with the help of an inmate. They told the inmate they would work something out for him in return for his cooperation.

The inmate who helped them was a young guy named Willie. He was in jail on a drug charge. He told them that his family would be bringing the money on their next visit. That afternoon Willie's family brought the money to him and investigators were waiting for him at the end of his visit. When they got Willie to their office, they made photocopies of all the money so they could use it as evidence against Starlyle: to make the conviction stick and to get her fired. After all the bills were marked and copied, they were returned to the inmate, and he was sent back to his dorm to wait for officer Starlyle to come in to work.

Shortly after Officer Starlyle arrived, Willie told her that he had the money and asked if she had the marijuana. She said that she did. About 3:30 p.m., they decided that Willie would walk out to the hallway and leave the brown bag with the money in it against the wall in the corner by the door. After Willie returned to the dorm, Officer Starlyle would go out to the hall and exchange the brown bag with the money in it for the bag that contained the marijuana.

That was when the investigators busted her: right after she put the marijuana down and picked up the money. Investigators rushed up on her and told her she was busted and would have to come with them to chief security. Chicago Police showed up at the chief security office shortly after they got Officer Starlyle there. The police officers read her Miranda rights to her and informed her that she was under arrest for selling drugs and bringing them into a penal institution. The investigators turned over the money, the marijuana, and the photocopies of the money, to the police. Chicago police officers then questioned Willie and told him that they would be in touch if they needed to ask him anything else. After a hearing with the County Merit Board, charges against Officer Starlyle were dropped in exchange for her willingness to resign from her job.

Officer Borden, a tall, thin Afro-American man, got busted for bringing drugs into the jail and for using drugs while on duty. One night, while he was supposed to be on duty, he left the dorm he was assigned to and was gone for almost two hours without a word to anyone about where he was going. When Officer Borden finally returned to his dorm, he was so messed up on the drugs he had taken that his dark hair was mussed and his brown eyes shone like glass. All he wanted to do was go to sleep. He decided to take one of the inmate's bunks and sleep for a while. The inmate who he threw out of the bunk was a young white guy in his early twenties named Paul. Paul had a very quiet disposition, and his blond hair and blue eyes made him look even younger than he was. Officer Borden told Paul to watch television while he slept and that Paul should wake him up just before five o'clock in the morning. Paul agreed to do it and went into the dayroom to watch the television.

Seeing as Officer Borden worked the midnight shift, he figured that his supervisor wouldn't come around and check on him. He couldn't have been more wrong. At around three o'clock, Sergeant Wolfe entered the dorm and asked Paul why he was still in the dayroom watching the television.

Paul told Sergeant Wolfe that Borden was tired and wanted to go to sleep for a few hours. He said Officer Borden had told him to go into the dayroom and watch television until a little before 5:00 a.m. and then come wake Borden up.

Sergeant Wolfe got very angry. He was a short, stocky man with large hands and a nasty disposition that showed in his dark-brown eyes. Wolfe walked back to the bunk that Officer Borden was sleeping on and noticed that all his clothes were in a pile on the floor with his shoes. Sergeant Wolfe left the dorm to get another brass member to witness Borden sleeping in the inmate's bed. According to the general orders, at least two brass members must witness an officer committing a major offense in order to discipline that officer.

When Sergeant Wolfe returned with Lieutenant Dome, they woke up Officer Borden and told him to get dressed and come to the security office immediately. By the time Borden arrived at the security office, Wolfe and Dome had already written him up for sleeping on the job, a major infraction.

A major infraction calls for an automatic twenty-nine-day suspension, pending termination after a hearing in front of the merit board. The hearing was held about a month after the incident, and Officer Borden had already been on suspension for the twenty-nine days. At the hearing, the board decided that because of the sleeping-on-duty incident, compounded by other disciplinary actions taken against Officer Borden just in the last year alone, he should be terminated. That is exactly what they did too.

Lieutenant Smithers, a tall, lanky man with dark eyes, dark hair, and a very nice disposition, was with the county approximately fifteen years when he was terminated for bringing drugs into the jail.

After months of suspecting that Smithers was bringing in drugs, investigators decided to watch his comings and goings at the jail. Anyone who left with him or spent any length of time with him was watched as well. Finally, one night after drugs were found on a dorm in Division One where Smithers was the supervisor, investigators thought it would be a good idea to set him up to see if he was really bringing drugs into the jail.

They enlisted the help of an inmate in the division who usually talked to Lieutenant Smithers. Sunny was an older man with thin brown hair, green eyes, and a reputation for using and selling drugs both inside the jail and out. The arrangement that was made between the investigators and Sunny was that he was supposed to listen and observe any conversations that took place between Lieutenant Smithers and any of the inmates in the division. After Sunny had any information, he was to contact the investigators, and they would take it from there.

About a week later, Sunny made the contact and told the investigators that he had overheard Lieutenant Smithers talking with an inmate about bringing in drugs in exchange for money from the inmate's family.

Investigations got all the information from Sunny on who the inmate was and where and how the deal would go down. The inmate was named Slick. His family was going to meet Lieutenant Smithers at Brown's Chicken Shack, a block from the jail, at 7:00 p.m. that Friday night.

On Friday, when Smithers arrived at work a little before 3:00 p.m., investigators started watching him. They continued to watch his every move until the time he left the jail to go for lunch. When Smithers walked out of the jail, investigators contacted chief security and told them to follow the lieutenant to the chicken place. When Lieutenant Smithers arrived at Brown's Chicken Shack, he waited outside for Slick's family to come and make the exchange. When they finally came outside, they got into Smither's car, but before they could finish the exchange, security personnel pulled up and told them to step out of the car and put their hands on the roof.

Once everyone was out of the car, they were frisked, read their Miranda rights, and taken to the closest police station for questioning. After everyone had been questioned, booked, and properly charged, they were taken to night court where their bail was paid.

Lieutenant Smithers paid his bail and left to go home. He had been told by security personnel that he couldn't return to work and that he would be notified by his superintendent as to when and if he could ever return to work.

After his hearing with the merit board and his day in court, Lieutenant Smithers was terminated from the county and given probation on the drug charge.

Officer Parks was very shifty when it came to doing his job. He was another officer busted for bringing drugs into the jail. He figured that because he had been with the county for almost twelve years he was beyond suspicion. He couldn't have been more wrong. He was already under suspicion of using drugs because of all the sick days he had the habit of taking. Officer Parks was using drugs for many years; however, it was just lately that it was taking a toll on him. His drug habit had aged him immensely. His bloodshot blue eyes and dirty-blond hair were telltale signs that his drug habit had become an addiction and was getting out of control.

Parks was using more drugs than he could afford. That's what made him decide to start selling drugs: to help supplement his income so he could afford his drug addiction. His big idea was to bring drugs into the jail in exchange for money from inmate's families.

He chose an inmate who he knew was in for a drug charge and would do anything to get drugs for his own use. The inmate Parks chose to deal with, on behalf of any other inmates interested, was a young guy named Ronnie. Ronnie was rather timid and had pretty much become the baby of the dorm. That just means he was the one who everyone looked out for so that nothing happened to him. Ronnie was perfect for the job in more ways than one, so investigators used him when it came to busting Officer Parks.

Investigations heard about Officer Parks through the jail's grapevine and decided to use an inmate to help bust him. It just so happened that they chose the same inmate as Parks had chosen to deal with. A coincidence or a setup? Most likely it was a setup. Investigators will use any means to trap an officer or a brass member suspected of bringing drugs into the jail even if it means using another officer to set them up.

When everything was set up between Ronnie and Officer Parks, investigators started to keep in touch with Ronnie on a daily basis. Ronnie told them when his family would be bringing in the money to exchange for the drugs. He told the investigators that his family would be coming to see him that Wednesday which was the dorm's regular visiting day.

Officer Parks worked the day shift. Ronnie's family usually came to see him around one o'clock in the afternoon and that Wednesday was no different.

A little after 1:00 p.m. on Wednesday, investigators met Ronnie's family in the visiting area. They gave the money to them long enough to mark the bills and make photocopies. Ronnie came to the visiting room to see his family and get the money from them.

He made sure that he didn't cut the visit any shorter than usual so Officer Parks wouldn't get suspicious. After Ronnie's visit was over, and he had returned to his dorm, Parks called him out to the hallway to make the exchange. Investigators had followed Ronnie back to his dorm. They wanted to bust Officer Parks while he was making the exchange with Ronnie. And that was exactly what they did! As soon as Officer Parks gave the drugs to Ronnie and had taken the money from him, Parks was surprised to see the investigators outside his dorm. Officer Parks was handcuffed, read his Miranda rights, and then taken to chief security to wait for Chicago Police to show up. When they finally arrived, they read him his rights again and took him to the police station to wait for his bail hearing.

That same night, Officer Parks was brought to night court, his bail was set, his wife paid it, and then he was sent home. He was not allowed to go back to work at the county until his hearing in front of the merit board. About three weeks after his arrest, he attended the hearing with the merit board. He was given the opportunity to resign and have the drug charges against him dropped. Officer Parks chose to resign and have the charges dropped. This left him with the future opportunity to get a decent job. He didn't receive any compensation for the time he was suspended.

The county deals with each officer pretty much the same way unless they have been in trouble before. Then they were terminated immediately, without a hearing and without pay or benefits.

CHAPTER 14

Discrimination or Favoritism

Any place of employment had problems with favoritism; and, most, if not all, places faced the problem of discrimination. The Cook County Jail was no exception to the rule! In the five years I'd been working at the county, I had seen more favoritism and discrimination than at any other job I'd ever had.

The first time I was a victim of discrimination at the jail was about six months after I started working for the county. I was assigned to Division Six for my first nine months with the county before I went into the training academy.

There was this female sergeant who worked the same shift I did, and she didn't like me one bit. Her name was Sergeant Kray; she was short, chubby, had reddish-brown hair and the meanest-looking brown eyes I'd ever seen. The first time I met her, she was very snobby toward me and said that she wouldn't tolerate any shit from anyone. What she should have said was that she didn't like white women and wouldn't put up with any shit from them. On the shift Kray and I worked, there were only a half a dozen white females in the division. Sergeant Kray didn't seem to like any of us—especially me.

I was only with the county about two and a half months when I had to have an emergency hysterectomy and appendectomy. About six weeks after the surgery, I returned to work because I didn't have any more sick time left. I was still a bit weak and needed to work a relatively easy assignment for a couple of weeks.

My lieutenant didn't have a problem with putting me in the security office or the interlock for a couple of weeks, but Kray did. When I requested the easier assignment for a couple of weeks, Sergeant Kray got really nasty with me and said that if I couldn't work my normal assignments, I had no business being back at work.

I got a bit upset and told her I didn't think she was being fair, and that I would appreciate it if she would at least think about it before she made any negative comments to me.

She got angry and told me that all she had to do was make a single phone call, and I would be back on medical leave. I told her to go ahead and try it. I would fight her every inch of the way.

I knew it was a case of discrimination because, a few months earlier, another female officer needed an easier assignment due to an injury, and she was given leave for almost a month. It just so happened that she was an Afro-American like Sergeant Kray. What a coincidence that turned out to be. Yeah, right, discrimination all the way no matter how you look at it.

Ever since that episode, Sergeant Kray tried to cause problems whenever she could. I was just a little bit smarter than her though. I had to make sure I stayed one step ahead of her at all times; that was the only thing that kept me from falling into her trap.

One time, she tried to get me in trouble with the supervisor of the training academy. She told me to stop in the security office of Division Six to pick up a time sheet for some overtime I had worked the week before I went into the academy. On my way out of the building, I stopped in the security office to pick up my time sheet. Sergeant Kray was sitting there waiting for me. As soon as I walked in, she started yelling at me and told me that I was in an unauthorized area. She said, "When you're in the academy, you aren't supposed to go to any other area of the jail but the training area." This was after she had told me to be there. What a bitch she was!

That gave her the opportunity to tell my supervisor that I went into a restricted area, then she would make sure that I got written up and reprimanded.

It didn't work out that way though. I went to my supervisor and explained to him what had happened. He said, "No problem. Just make sure that from now on, you don't go into any unauthorized areas while you're in the training academy."

Sergeant Kray wasn't very happy with me after that; in fact, she tried even harder to mess with me. It didn't work, though, because I knew what she was up to.

Once, when Officer Gluzsek needed a few days off work for a family emergency, she was told she couldn't have the time off. When officer Carnes needed a few emergency medical days off, he was given them with no problems. Officer Gluzsek, who was white and not liked by the captain in the division, had gone straight to the captain's office with tears in her brown eyes and asked the captain for the time off. Officer Gluzsek was very sincere in her explanation as to why she needed the time off.

Her father was terminally ill and wasn't expected to live much longer. She was so stressed and grief-stricken about her father that she was twirling her fingers through her short dark hair. Officer Carnes who, on the other hand, was an Afro-American didn't bother to come in at all. He just called the captain's office, asked for the time off, and was given it without any questions asked. Captain Bully was an Afro-American man and so was Officer Carnes. (Not to mention the fact that Carnes and Captain Bully talked a lot and got along really good with each other.) Some might have said it was favoritism, and some may have said it was discrimination. Personally, I believe it was another case of discrimination.

Officer Kramer, a white female officer in Division Eight, had a car accident and was badly injured. She almost lost one of her beautiful blue eyes when her windshield was shattered in the accident. Because of her tiny bone structure, she was thrown from the seat of the car into the dash and split her head open. This left her light-brown hair matted with blood. Because of the time of the accident, no one was able to notify the county until the time she was scheduled to start work. The county tried to mark her down as absent, no call. But when Officer Matson, an Afro-American who had a car accident and didn't call in and ask for medical leave until almost two hours after he was scheduled to start work, he was given special consideration. Favoritism or discrimination? A clear-cut case of discrimination!

The majority (95 percent) of the county was made up of African-Americans; then there was the small percentage left (5 percent) split among Hispanics, Whites, Orientals, and mixed nationalities. In the five years I had been with the county, I had yet to see any one of any nationality get the same treatment or even close to the same treatment as an Afro-American person received from authority figures. Discrimination was something that should never be allowed in the workplace, no matter where that workplace was or what type of employment it offered. All employees should be treated equally, no matter what nationality they were, males or females, smart or not very intelligent. Whether a person was liked or not was no reason to discriminate against that person. Everyone deserved a chance at all the different jobs within the county jail, not just the individuals who were part of the in-crowd.

CHAPTER 15

Administration

The administrative personnel at the Cook County Jail lacked compassion and thoughts of safety where the officers were concerned.

Most places of employment had pretty decent administrative people as well as not-so-decent people. Unfortunately, the Cook County Sheriffs Department had more flaws than assets. The county's administrative staff were pretty much selected by the sheriff and the director of the jail. If they were voted into their positions, maybe we would have a better administrative staff.

Whenever an officer or any member of the correctional department wished to speak with someone in the administration department regarding the working conditions at the jail, they had to go through all kinds of red tape. The first thing we were expected to do was contact our immediate supervisor and explain what our situation was, then our supervisor will contact his supervisor; he, in turn, must contact the division's superintendent to explain the situation. Only after everyone had been notified, and if our request was deemed necessary, can we finally get up to the administrative level.

You would think after all the shit we had to go through to get there, they would at least be a little considerate and cooperative with us. Not the county! It didn't matter to them how much bullshit we went through. If they didn't want to listen to us or try to help us through the problem, they won't.

The first time I had ever dealt with the administration at the jail was when I needed to take time off work during April of 1990.

I thought that it would always be easy to deal with the jail's director. What a surprise I was in for after the new director took over. I had only been with the county for a little over three months when I needed to have a hysterectomy and get my appendix taken out. The first thing I was told to do was to write a memo to my immediate supervisor, and he would pass it on to the superintendent of my division. By the time the director of the jail received the memo, I only had one week left until I had to go into the hospital for surgery.

At that time, we had Director Leak in charge of the jail. He gave me the time off as a medical emergency and said that it was excused sick time. That way, it wouldn't be held against me when our performance evaluations were done. When I finally got around to talking to Director Leak, he was very understanding about my need for time off. He told me that he hoped everything went well and that I should take my time to heal properly before returning to work. Director Leak was a really decent person who cared about all his employees at the county. He also believed in an open-door policy for all of us.

That was the way all directors should run things in the administration department: treat your employees with respect and consideration, then they will feel like doing a better job. Increased self-esteem, and job performance increases; lowered self-esteem, and you'll have poor work performance.

Not all directors agreed with those methods, though, especially not the new director who came to the county jail late in November of 1990. What a bastard he turned out to be! Director Fairlane and his staff were of the belief that you treat employees as if they were lower than the inmates. If an officer wanted to speak to anyone on the administrative level, he or she had to go through so much bullshit and red tape that a lot of officers gave up trying to get an appointment with the director.

Then of course, there were those officers who never give up. I was one such officer. One time, while I was on vacation, the captain of my division said that I didn't actually have three vacation days that I had taken. So while I was in Arizona vacationing with my kids and my husband, I was being marked down as absent, no call for three days in a row. When I got back from my vacation, there was a message on my answering machine from the captain of my division. The message said that I needed to contact personnel immediately.

When I got home and unpacked, I tried to contact personnel to straighten out the miscalculation of my vacation time. After calling three or four times and asking to speak with the timekeeper for my division, I finally got through to her, but we couldn't seem to resolve the problem. After all the time I had wasted trying to get through to personnel, I reached a dead end.

When I tried to see the director, in hopes of resolving the problem, I was told to go through the proper channels first. Thusly came all the bullshit.

In the county, the proper procedure was to speak with your sergeant, then your lieutenant, then your captain and finally, the superintendent of your division. If you didn't get the results you wanted after going through the proper chain of command, you will try to get an appointment with the director. After almost a week of red tape, I finally got my appointment with the director. Unfortunately, I was in and out of his office in less than five minutes. During that time, I really didn't feel that he heard a word I was saying to him. Every time I tried to show him the pink slip—I had signed by my captain, and the superintendent of the division—he said that it didn't matter what I had: the records in the personnel office stated that I didn't have enough vacation days on the books at the time I went on my vacation. Of course, he wouldn't even listen to the possibility that personnel had made a mistake when calculating my vacation time. That would have been the easy thing to do. But the county didn't seem to do things the easy way ever!

Finally, I went back to the personnel department and insisted on going through my file with the timekeeper for my division. I wanted to see it for myself. I brought in my records of the time that I should have had on the books, and we compared it with the time personnel had on their books. I was relieved to find out they had made an error in the addition of my time when they carried over my days from the end of the prior year to the new year's figures.

The thing about the whole incident that bothered me the most was the fact that not one person involved would admit they were wrong or even offered me any kind of apology. The timekeeper for my division just said that we were all human and mistakes can be made. Furthermore, Captain Bully threw out all the original copies he had written about my three absent days. From that point on Captain Bully messed with me and tried his best to make my job miserable.

As for Director Fairlane, he didn't even bother to say anything to me about what happened. I know for a fact, though, that if I hadn't found the mistake, he would have gladly signed the write-ups and suspended me.

The main thing I'd learned about the administration at the Cook County Jail was that they were not conscientious people. They just didn't give a damn about their officers or the civilians who worked there. All the administrators worried about was themselves; nobody else's feelings or thoughts mattered one bit to them. I guess you could say that the officers and other staff members at the jail were just employees to them; we were not even considered to be human.

The next time I had the misfortune of dealing with the county's administration was when I got written up by a sergeant from the chief security department. I was working at the Scan Ray, a security checkpoint in the Cermak Hospital, when the sergeant came through on his hourly check and saw me playing a Nintendo Game Boy. Boy, was he pissed off at me! He looked at my badge and my name tag then left the area to notify my supervisor of what he had just observed. Approximately twenty minutes later, I was called to the security office of my division. My sergeant and my captain were both there when I arrived. All I could think was that I was in deep shit.

All my sergeant could think to say to me was, "Officer Wilkinson, what the hell did you think you were doing? You know you're not allowed to bring games to the jail to use during your tour of duty."

I told him that I had gotten bored just sitting there with nothing to do after things had slowed down, so I decided to find something to keep me busy so I wouldn't fall asleep and then get written up for sleeping on the job.

Fine job I did in trying not to get written up. I got written up for inattention to duty, which wasn't a major offense. It was to me, though, because now it was in my file, and I had never been written up for anything before.

Seeing as I couldn't talk them out of the write-up, I requested a hearing with the merit board to fight it. I just felt fair was fair. Why write me up when you won't write up another officer for doing the very same thing?

When I finally had my hearing, I had to deal with the administration, once again. What a pain in the ass that was. The time of the hearing was supposed to be 9:00 a.m., but I didn't get called in until almost eleven thirty. Talk about being behind schedule.

All hearings were held before a merit board. The board was made up of three officers from different areas of the jail: one captain, one lieutenant, and the superintendent of your own division.

While I was waiting for my hearing to begin, one of the union stewards for the county came in to speak with me. Officer Gates was a very intelligent Afro-American woman with short dark hair and lively green eyes that always seemed to sparkle when she smiled. She had been with the county for many years and helped a lot of officers when it came to getting proper representation at their hearings. Officer Gates told me to admit to playing the Game Boy and request that my write-up be thrown out just as had been done for several other officers who were caught playing Game Boys by the same supervisor.

In other words, I felt that there was a case of favoritism where the other officers were concerned and maybe even a bit of sexual discrimination. I was a woman, and the other officers were all men.

When I finally went into the room for my hearing, I explained what had happened and then expressed that I felt it was a case of the supervisor not liking me. Why else would he have written me up and not the others?

The merit board decided to change my write-up to a written reprimand with no suspension days. What a relief that was! I thought, for sure, I was going to get screwed.

In more cases than not, the county's administration department will not offer any special consideration for an officer who had been written up by a well-liked supervisor. If you want or need any special consideration, the county's administration was definitely not the place to go looking for it.

CHAPTER 16

Disability Leave

All places of employment have a workman's compensation benefits for their employees when they are hurt on the job. Not all companies recognize mental stress caused by a job as meriting compensatory payment. According to the county, the state of Illinois doesn't recognize mental stress as a work-related injury at any place of employment. This was exactly the problem I ran into with the county in September and October of 1994.

Over a brief period of time, before my last day at work, I had many things happen on the dorms I worked: inmate fights, staff shortages, and harassment from my supervisors and coworkers. All this contributed to my being off-work and on disability. Some of the main contributing factors were: a really bad fight between two inmates on a dorm one night, another fight involving two inmates where one of the inmates convinced an officer to side with him against me, and on the last night I worked, I was locked in a cell with fighting inmates for approximately thirty minutes.

In September of 1994, while I was working dorm B3 in the RTU building of Division Eight, two inmates started fighting over a dinner tray. The two inmates were Rodney and Alphonso. Rodney used his height, along with his large, rugged build, to intimidate Alphonso into doing what he wanted him to do. Alphonso was shorter than Rodney and less aggressive, yet he could be very violent when provoked. Alphonso's dark green eyes glared with anger whenever Rodney got near him.

Finally, one night in September, Alphonso snapped; he just couldn't take any more of Rodney's abuse. This time, when Rodney picked a fight with him, he fought back.

Rodney was the kind of inmate who always messed with any inmate he felt superior to or just didn't like. On this particular night, he got more than what he bargained for when he messed with Alphonso.

The dinner trays had just been delivered to the dorm. Rodney told Alphonso that he wanted food from Alphonso's tray and that he'd best back off and leave him alone. One thing led to another, and the next thing I knew, the two inmates were fighting with each other. Rodney threw the first punch and connected with Alphonso's head, throwing him off balance. Once Alphonso cleared his head, he lunged at Rodney, grabbing him around the neck. He was trying to wrestle Rodney to the floor when Rodney bit his thumb, almost severing it from the hand. There was blood spurting everywhere.

That's when I got tired of yelling for the officer across the hall to come over and help me. I felt, at that point, I had no other choice but to try to break up the fight myself. What a mistake that was! Rodney tried to hit me with a chair, but I ducked. Another inmate named Jimmy saw what was happening and jumped in to help me. As soon as he grabbed for Rodney, they both fell onto one of the bunks and Jimmy broke his hand. Jimmy was not a very large man, but he did have a lot of determination and compassion for the officers who he liked. Thank God, I was one he liked.

By the time other officers and brass finally arrived on the dorm, the fight was already over. Rodney had a broken nose, Alphonso's thumb on his left hand was partially severed from his hand, and Jimmy's hand was broken. All three inmates needed immediate medical attention. They also needed to speak with their psyche workers about their states of mind.

I was pretty shook up over the fight myself: all that blood all over the place! It wasn't easy trying to keep the rest of the dorm under control and break up the fight without any help from any other officers.

After everything was settled, the dorm was cleaned up, and I sat down to write my report on the incident. My supervisor came back to the dorm and reamed me out for calling for backup. According to the brass, the only reason an officer should call for assistance was if they were getting hurt or were hurt. I really think that was a stupid way of looking at it because I felt my physical well-being was in jeopardy, and that was why I called for assistance. I would do it again!

After Rodney and Alphonso got back from Cermak Medical Center, they were both put in isolation for three hours. When they returned to the dorm, they were told to stay on their bunks until the end of the shift.

Jimmy didn't return to the dorm until the next day because he had to have his hand set and put into a cast. He was in pretty good spirits when I saw him the next day. To thank him for what he had done to help me the night before, when I went out for lunch, I got him a nice juicy hamburger with all the fixings on it. He really enjoyed that a lot. It was the least I could do to show my appreciation for his help. The brass didn't agree with my way of thinking though. Tough shit! I did, and that was all that matters.

The next incident took place on October 13, 1994, at 7:45 p.m., just as I was returning from lunch. When I entered the drug unit of Division Eight, I saw two inmates from my dorm standing by the security office with my sergeant.

When I asked what was going on, my sergeant told me that the two inmates, Charles and James, were fighting over packets of sugar. Since I couldn't get any straight answers out of Charles or James, I decided to go back upstairs to the dorm and question some of the other inmates hoping to get the full story.

After speaking with several inmates who had seen and heard what took place, I was able to find out that James had some sugar in his cell, and he didn't want to give it to Charles who had asked for some to put in his coffee. Charles grabbed the sugar out of James's hand with his huge knuckled hand and said that now James wasn't going to get shit either. Pissed off by what Charles had done, James followed him all the way down the full length of the cells, yelling at him to give him back his fucking sugar. Then he knocked Charles's coffee out of his hand and pushed him up against the wall.

After several attempts on Charles's part to avoid James's anger, he finally got pissed off and told James to leave him alone, or he would fuck him up. James didn't take Charles seriously, and he pushed him up against the wall again. That was when Charles let him have it. He used his thin, bony hand to punch James, breaking his nose. Blood was spurting everywhere scaring some of the other inmates. Instantly, you could see James's brown eyes turn black and blue then becoming glassy and swollen.

By the time the officer working the dorm (I was at lunch) realized what was happening and removed the two inmates from the dorm, the damage was already done.

Both inmates received write-ups, were removed from the drug unit, taken to Cermak to get medical attention, and then were put in isolation until the end of the shift. Gateway staff, the people in charge of the inmates in the drug unit, talked with both inmates and then had them transferred to different divisions. As a result of Charles's and James's actions, neither one of them was allowed to continue with the drug program or go to a halfway house to get the treatment they really needed.

Later that same night, the final incident took place on the same dorm with two other inmates. I went in the dorm to lock up the cells for the night around 10:30 p.m. like usual, only this night didn't turn out to be a usual one. I had locked up all the cells with the exception of one, cell three, and that was where I ended up having problems.

Inmates Perry and Wayne were housed in that cell together. They were supposed to be good friends, but I sure couldn't tell that from the way they were acting. Something was definitely wrong between them on that particular night.

As I approached their cell, I could hear them arguing about commissary items that were missing from their cell. Perry was yelling that Wayne had stolen his commissary to take with him the following day when he was to be shipped to the state prison.

Wayne claimed he hadn't taken Perry's stuff and that Perry couldn't prove he had. As things progressed, Perry became quieter and said, "The hell with it. It doesn't matter if I get my shit back or not."

Wayne, on the other hand, was becoming more defiant in his behavior. He took three containers of roll-on deodorant, stuffed them into a large white sock, and tied a big knot in it. I couldn't believe Wayne would make a weapon in front of me and not even thought about the consequences he faced. I really didn't think he cared what would happen to him or to me.

I told Wayne several times to put the weapon down or to at least turn it over to me, but he refused saying, "I ain't giving you the fucking weapon. If you want it, you'll have to take it from me." At that point, I was pretty pissed off, but I was also scared, so I just grabbed the weapon from Wayne and told him that he was in deep shit now.

About a minute or two later, Perry stepped in between the two of us, giving me the opportunity to get the hell out of there and back to the dayroom where the other officer would be able to see me.

When I got to the door, the officer let me out. Then he said, "What the hell took you so long? I was beginning to wonder what had happened to you." (He just wasn't concerned enough to send someone in to check on me.)

I told him that, since he was sitting in the chair at the monitor, he should have known what was going on in there. He told me that he couldn't see me or hear anything I was saying because the intercom and the monitor were broken. It was at that point I remembered we had told our sergeant at the beginning of our shift that the monitor and intercom system were not working. That just made me even more upset; how the hell can the county expect us to work in an unsafe environment? It was obvious they didn't give a shit!

After I contacted my supervisor and had the two inmates taken off the dorm, I sat down to write the report on what had just taken place. I was pretty shaky, feeling sick to my stomach, and had an excruciating headache. Because my hands were shaking so bad, I had trouble writing. It took me about an hour to write up the reports and get them signed by my supervisor.

Around 11:30 p.m., my husband came into the security office to see what was taking so long. He was really surprised when my supervisor told him about what had happened on the second floor of the drug unit.

After I finished the paperwork, I filled out my overtime slip and had my supervisor sign it. Then he had to have the superintendent of the division sign it as well so it would be valid.

I finally got out of work about midnight, totally exhausted, mentally and physically, and sick to my stomach. By the time I got home, I was throwing up and ended up spending most of the night in the bathroom. I tried to sleep for a while, but I couldn't. I kept having the same nightmare every time I'd close my eyes: inmates fighting and one has a weapon.

The sleeplessness continued for the first couple of weeks that I was home from work. The nightmares were a constant part of my days and nights for weeks. Part of my anxiety stemmed from the fact that the day after the incident in the drug unit, the lieutenant of the division—knowing that the other night affected me—wanted to put me back in the same spot again even though the equipment still wasn't working. I went to see a therapist and a psychiatrist at the recommendation of the Employee Assistance Program (EAP). They thought some therapy might help me feel better and get me out of my major depression.

By this time, I had gone through all the red tape required by the county to explain what had happened at work on October 13, as well as on the day I had tried to return to work only three days later. After filing one paper after another and making phone call after phone call, I was told that the county probably wouldn't accept my claim for having suffered work-related injuries.

Of course, I was pretty pissed off. Who the hell did they think they were? Telling me that my claim had nothing to do with my job at the county. It sure the hell did!

The person who I spoke with the most was a man named Dan Mailer. He was with the county safety board. I met him in person after I had spoken with him on the phone several times. The first few times I spoke with Dan, he wasn't very friendly or compassionate about what I was going through. After the sixth time that we spoke on the phone, he told me that if the county ruled in my favor about my claim, he and several other employees would be off work the very next day due to work-related stress. I thought that was a really rotten thing for him to say to me, especially when he didn't have all the facts nor did he even want to listen to them!

A couple of days after the last time we spoke, a woman named Wanda Haze called me to say that Dan Mailer had asked her to call and make an appointment.

Wanda came out to my house a week later to give me a psychiatric evaluation and talked to me about what had happened on my last day of work.

She was a really nice lady with dark-brown hair that accentuated her green eyes. Wanda spent about four hours with me. She asked me all kinds of questions about what had happened: how I felt at the time of the incident, how I had been feeling since then, how I was feeling right then while we were talking, and why I thought I was feeling the things I was feeling. I got a bit upset and was getting even more depressed while we were talking.

The worst part of the whole interview was when I had to relive what had happened on my last night of work. It made me feel scared again. It also made me feel helpless and like a little girl: one who didn't have any control of the situation or any way out of a trap. It was like someone else was making events in your life happen, and there was nothing you can do to prevent it or change it. Anxiety, frustration, helplessness, and sheer exhaustion were the main things I felt for weeks when I was home from work. I had daily headaches, an upset stomach, nervous shakes, as well as nightmares about being trapped in a closed area with no way out.

By the time Wanda was done talking with me and was ready to leave, she told me that she felt that my situation met the requirements for workman's compensation. I asked her if that was what her recommendation was going to be to Dan Mailer and to the safety board. She told me that she was going to tell them the same thing she had told me.

The next day, I spoke with Dan on the phone again. He was still acting very nasty toward me. In our phone conversation Dan told me that the decision of the board would be not to pay my claim.

He didn't feel that it fell within the guidelines of the workman's compensation plan.

I again tried to tell him about everything that had contributed to the mental stress, in addition to what had happened at work on October 13, 1994.

Dan Mailer still wasn't interested in hearing my side of things. He just kept saying that I didn't have any proof of my allegations. The reason he thought that was because he wouldn't listen to what I was trying to say to him, and he hadn't read the reports that were written either.

By the time we got off the phone, I was very upset and in tears: partly out of frustration and partly discouragement. For the rest of the day, I couldn't concentrate on much of anything. I had a really bad headache and was sick to my stomach again. I couldn't believe any one human being could be so unfeeling when it came to another person's life and livelihood.

It was at that point that I decided I needed to contact a lawyer to see if I had a legal suit against the county. I talked with Attorney Kevin Millon, and he told me that he thought I had a good case. Kevin also told me to bring him all the reports I had written regarding the incident on the night of October 13, 1994, and any other reports and/or paperwork I had that would substantiate my claim against the county.

When I met with Kevin Millon in person, for the first time, he looked over all the papers I had brought with me. We then talked for about an hour and a half, and then he told me that he felt I had an excellent chance to win my case against the county.

A week later, Wanda Haze called to tell me she had just met with Dan Mailer and that after they finished talking he had asked her to call me. The purpose of the phone call was for Wanda to tell me that Dan was really sorry about how our phone conversation went a week ago. He said that he really didn't have all the facts or knew all the circumstances of my situation when he told me there was no way the county would pay my claim.

About an hour or so after Wanda and I got off the phone, Dan called to tell me he was sorry about the way he treated me when we spoke last. He also wanted me to know that he had set up an appointment with a psychiatrist named Dr. Ganellon for January 30, 1995, at one o'clock in the afternoon. The purpose of the appointment was so that the county would have two professionals who agreed on the diagnosis required for me to receive the workman's compensation.

The week before I was to have my appointment with Dr. Ganellon, the county gave me my first check for the first three months that I was off work. Dan Mailer told me that I would be receiving a check every two weeks and that the checks would continue until I was released by my doctor to return to work. If I was not able to return to the county in the same capacity as before, then I would be compensated by the safety board with a tax-free check equal to what my income would be if I still worked as a correctional officer. I was told to be at the doctor's office no later than 1:00 p.m. so that I would have enough time to complete all the tests.

On the day that the appointment was originally scheduled, Dr. Ganellon had to cancel because he was very sick with the flu. I tried for the remainder of that week to get hold of him, or someone in his office, to reschedule my appointment, but I didn't have any luck reaching him. Wanda Haze and Dan Mailer kept in touch with me, and the three of us kept leaving messages for Dr. Ganellon to call any one of us as soon as he returned to work.

I finally heard something from Dr. Ganellon the following week. We scheduled an appointment for Thursday, February 9, 1995, at 9:30 a.m.

On Tuesday, February 7, Dr. Ganellon called to cancel our appointment for that Thursday. He wanted to reschedule it for the following Monday at 1:00 p.m. I told him that it wasn't a good day for me and that we would have to schedule it on another day. We discussed when it would be mutually satisfactory for both us and decided on Wednesday, March 1, 1995. During the course of our conversation, I informed Dr. Ganellon that I had a family emergency and would be going out of the state for two weeks.

Dr. Ganellon didn't seem to have a problem with that although Dan Mailer did. I called Dan Mailer to let him know that Dr. Ganellon had canceled again and that we were unable to reschedule the appointment until Wednesday, March 1. Dan asked me why it was going to be so long until the appointment, and I explained that I had a family emergency. He told me that it was quite unusual for someone on disability from work to be out of the state. Furthermore, he did not feel that I should be paid my disability benefits during the two-week period I would be gone from my home.

After I got off the phone, I contacted my attorney, Kevin Millon, who told me that the county had no right to arbitrarily withhold my benefits because of my family situation. Kevin and I discussed the details of the family emergency. He told me to just proceed as I'd planned, to do what I needed to do, as long as it wouldn't interfere with my therapy sessions with any of my doctors.

I informed Kevin that my next appointments with my doctors weren't until February 27 and March 6 and that I wouldn't miss either one of them because of the trip.

Even though Dan Mailer had told me that my disability benefits would not be discontinued after my appointment with Dr. Ganellon, my benefits were discontinued shortly after I went out of State.

I contacted Dan as soon as I got back from my trip. He didn't say anything to me about my benefits ending, only that I wouldn't be paid for the time I was gone.

My attorney finally told me that my benefits were discontinued until Dr. Ganellon saw me, and he also informed Dan Mailer that my condition was due to my job. The county now felt that, due to my past medical history, my condition had nothing to do with the job; therefore, they shouldn't have to issue any further disability checks.

Around the end of February, I was informed by a black female officer (who wishes to remain anonymous) that she had just returned to work after being on mental-stress leave for the past five and a half months. She also informed my husband that she was also hassled by the county when she was on disability and once her benefits started they were not discontinued until after she had returned to work. Once again, here was different treatment for one officer as opposed to another. I see it as another case of discrimination by the county.

I spoke with my attorney and informed him of the new development. It was added to the file against the county. According to Kevin Millon, it could still take at least six more months before I would start to receive my disability checks again. In that time frame, I would have more financial stress because of my lack of income which, in turn, would make my case against the county even stronger. I had a car payment to make each month, as well as a mortgage payment, not to mention utilities and food money. The county was to blame for anything that I had lost as a result of them stopping my benefits while I was still under the care of two doctors. Both doctors agreed that I was not ready to return to my job at the county.

Once again, my financial fate was in the hands of another doctor who worked for the county. That was a real bad feeling to have: you feel helpless.

My appointment with Dr. Ganellon took approximately five and a half hours from start to finish. I was kind of nervous when I first arrived. I didn't know this person who I was going to be discussing some of my innermost thoughts and feelings with. Before the appointment took place, Dr. Ganellon told me that he would be conducting a variety of tests consisting of comprehension, inkblot, emotional awareness, how I perceived different pictures of different situations, etc. I figured, by the time we finished with the appointment, he would know just about everything there was to know about me; and I still wouldn't know anything about him. It really gave me an uneasy feeling to tell him so much about me and yet to know so little about him. All that meant to me was that the county would try to use the information I had given to Dr. Ganellon against me at a later date.

Dr. Ganellon's main concern was my past and my childhood rather than the incident at the jail that caused me to leave my job. After almost two hours of questioning me about my past, Dr. Ganellon was ready to move on to the next phase of his testing. He didn't seem to want to discuss the situation at the jail or what had really caused my mental stress. I had to keep bringing up the incident at the jail. Finally, Dr. Ganellon listened to me and asked me questions about what had happened on the night of October 13, 1994—my last night at work.

During the time we talked, he didn't seem to take very seriously the incident at the jail. In fact, he seemed to be taking it rather lightly. Dr. Ganellon didn't think that verbal threats along with a weapon being waved at me were all that traumatic. I told him that it was to me, especially seeing as I was the one who was stuck in the cell with the two inmates for at least thirty minutes with no one to back me up or help me. The panic and fear I felt was very overwhelming. I was afraid for my safety as well as felt very helpless. I didn't think I would ever get out of that cell area in one piece. That was the longest thirty minutes I'd ever spent during my whole five years of working for the county.

After I completed all the tests for Dr. Ganellon, he talked with me for a few more minutes. He asked if I had any paperwork with me that would substantiate my claim of what had happened on my last night at work. I told him that I did. I took everything out of the envelope I had brought with me and gave Dr. Ganellon reports that were filed on the incident. I showed him pictures that were drawn by officers, expressing their opinions of my husband and me. I showed him the reports that I had written to my supervisor, as well as to the superintendent of Division Eight, and statements from inmates involved in an earlier fight on the same night of the incident that caused me to take temporary disability leave. I got the strong impression Dr. Ganellon didn't feel my claim had much merit.

The last part of the testing involved a booklet with 567 questions pertaining to my feelings about different people, job possibilities, habits, mental state, sleeping, eating, and social habits since the incident at work. A lot of the questions were repetitive: probably to see if they could catch me in a lie or maybe just to confuse me. Unfortunately for him, I was pretty observant. I had nothing to hide, so my story never changed.

In one part of the test, the doctor showed me several pictures and asked me to tell him what the pictures meant to me. I thought this was rather strange, but I did as he requested. The first picture I was shown consisted of a little boy sitting on the floor by a bench, with his head on it, crying. I told Dr. Ganellon I thought the little boy was upset about something and might be feeling like he was alone.

The next picture was of a woman with a little girl. They both looked like they were upset. I thought the little girl had done something wrong, and her mother was scolding her.

The picture that followed was of a man farming in a large field, a woman holding some books, and a woman standing by a tree with her hands crossed on her stomach. I told Dr. Ganellon I thought the man was trying to farm his land to make a good living for his family; the woman with the books was attending college; and the woman standing by the tree was the mother, and she was in charge of the household chores.

Then we moved along to the inkblot test that had to be the dumbest one of all. Dr. Ganellon showed me several inkblot pictures of various shapes, sizes, and colors. He then asked me to tell him what kinds of animals I saw in the inkblots.

After I completed all the tests, the doctor and I talked for a few minutes. He told me it would be at least ten to fourteen days before his report would be typed up and sent to Dan Mailer and to my attorney Kevin Millon.

All that meant to me was that it would be at least four more weeks until I received another disability check; that is if the county decided to reinstate my benefits.

When I spoke to my attorney about all the bullshit, he told me that he had already filed a 19 B petition: a petition to try to get back all my benefits from the county. Kevin said that I would have to wait approximately six more months to go through all the red tape with the courts unless the county decided to cooperate with us and reinstate my disability benefits. According to my attorney, there was an arbitrator called in to help the county decide what their responsibility to me was regarding the incident at the jail on October 13, 1994. Attorney Millon informed me that he thought it would be a good idea for me to see if my doctor would give me a release to look for another job.

On March 6, 1995, I went to see Dr. Dubinski, the psychiatrist who I had been seeing since I went on disability. She told me that she did not feel it would be in my best interest to return to my current position at the county. Her expert opinion was that I try to find a job in one of the other fields in which I had worked before I started working for the Cook County Sheriffs Department.

I had experience in computers, word processing, bookkeeping, accounting, accounts payable and receivable, as well as being skilled in customer relations and administrative assistance in an insurance company.

Once again, I was back in the grind of looking for a job. I really thought I was done looking for a new career. I guess not! I set up three interviews with different companies in the next week, hoping one of them would be the start of a new career for me. From what I saw in the employment ads, none of the positions being offered paid nearly as much as what I was making at the county. Then again, I supposed that, in time, the pay would increase to a more substantial scale.

It was really a shame that a person can't get a job, do an honest day's work, take home a paycheck, and have his or her life run smoothly. All I ever wanted was to work, make a good home, raise my two boys, have a successful marriage, and live a comfortable financial existence. Is that really too much to ask out of life? I didn't think it was!

As far as the county was concerned, it was. They were always fucking with someone's livelihood. If it was not with an officer, it was with one of the civilians or an inmate. Life is too short to sweat the small shit. But this was not what I considered to be small shit. That was why I retained an attorney to fight them. It may take a few weeks, a few months, or even a few years, but I was not the type of person to sit by and let anyone fuck with me, my family, or anyone else I cared about.

EPILOGUE

On Thursday, October 13, 1994, I was involved in a traumatic incident on the second floor of the drug unit in Division Eight.

Although it only lasted for thirty minutes, it still left lasting scars. It took me months to get over it enough to even think about returning to the workforce. What made it even harder for me to get over was the fact that the administration within the county gave me such a hard time and hassled me every step of the way. I started seeing a therapist as well as a psychiatrist immediately. All I wanted to do was get the help I needed to overcome the trauma I had suffered so I could return to work.

After several months of pain, suffering, hassles with the county, doctors' appointments on a regular basis, bill collectors yelling at me that they wanted their money, and fights with my husband about our lack of money to live on, the county finally decided to pay me my disability benefits.

After more than a week of trying to get in touch with Dan Mailer, I finally called my attorney to see what, if anything, we could do at that point to get my benefits reinstated.

It was at that point that I was informed why my benefits were stopped. According to Kevin, the county had stopped my benefits because of my past history of emotional problems: two bad marriages, one a very violent one, the other ended just after my two children were born.

After the second marriage broke up, my first husband decided to take the two children to live with him in California. That was very traumatic for me, but not to the point that the county wanted to believe. All they wanted to do was to push the blame off themselves and on to everyone else. The county never took responsibility for its mistakes unless they were forced to by the courts. Even then, they tried to fight it for as long as they could.

Kevin Millon thought that it would be in my best interest to start looking for another job just as soon as my two doctors released me from disability. I took his advice because he said that it was the best way to handle the situation at that point in time. More so, as the county was still trying to question my willingness to search for work.

It was very frustrating for me to be back out there looking for a job again after five years at the county. I really forgot what it was like out there: going through the grind of looking for the right job with the type of pay I felt I was worth as well as entitled to. It seemed that for every job advertised, there were at least two hundred applicants. Not very good odds, no matter how you look at it. One of the jobs that I applied for drew over five hundred applicants to fill only ten positions. The callback rate was only 15 percent; unfortunately, I wasn't one of them.

I began to realize that being a Cook County deputy sheriff for the last five years didn't carry a whole lot of weight in the working world. In fact, I got the feeling from a couple of places that it actually hurt my chances of getting that particular job. It was really strange how some jobs listed on a resume were an asset for future jobs, while others were considered to be liabilities. I wonder why that is?

I was still seeing my therapist, as well as my psychiatrist, Dr. Dubinski. This was mostly for moral support during the weeks ahead while looking for a new job and fighting the county in court.

Out of the last five months, there had only been one month that I was free of the constant stress of wondering how I would pay my bills and put food on the table. For five years, I had not had to worry about how I was going to pay my bills. Then, in a flash, I was struggling and wondering where my next meal was going to come from. That really took a toll on a person, emotionally as well as physically, not to mention how it affected everyone else in your household.

Besides job hunting, I'd been working on assignments for my writing class as well as this book. So many things to do and so little time to do them in.

The county was so engrossed in fighting to hold on to its money that it forgot how to care for people who worked for it as well as their families. At one time, these people must have cared about someone else; they all had families of their own.

The only person who I felt ever cared about my situation, besides my psychiatrist, was my attorney. At least, the attorney tried to help me as best he could.

I spent the next six months or so fighting one court battle after another against the county. At the end of the six months, there had to be a resolution to the problem one way or another hopefully in my favor and not the county's.

After five years of dedicated service to the Cook County Sheriffs Department, the least they could do for me was to cover my disability for the length of time the doctors felt I needed to be off work. Originally, the doctors felt I would only need to be off work for a few months, but that was before all the shit happened with the county.

I went through different phases of depression from October of 1994 and onward. The first phase lasted for almost two months. The sleepless nights and the crying spells were the worst part of it all. It was so bad that I couldn't eat or get through the day without a headache. The sleepless nights just made the days seem even longer, especially when you didn't feel good, and you're under a lot of stress.

Doctor Dubinski thought it would be a good idea to increase my Prozac from 20 mg to 40 mg each day. That turned out not to be such a good idea; it just made my headaches much more severe. After a month or so, she decided to take me off the Prozac and tried a new drug called Zoloft. She prescribed 50 mg to start with. I was on the Zoloft about a month when I noticed that my headaches had decreased considerably. I only had them once every couple of days. I was sleeping a little better as well. Since the medication was helping me, Dr. Dubinski told me to keep taking it until I felt I didn't need it any more. As it turned out, I was still taking that medication.

The only drawback to the medication, in the beginning, was that it made me feel extremely drowsy in the morning, and I gained a few pounds. I've had my good days and bad days since I started taking the medication, but I do feel it has made a difference in my emotional state.

I wasn't the first officer to take time off work for stress-related reasons. There had been many other officers who have had things happen to them while they worked at the county that caused them emotional problems. In each of those cases, where the officers chose to seek psychiatric help, the county fought them all the way. A couple of them retained lawyers and sued the county. As far as I have been able to find out, they had all finally won their cases after a long hard fight.

Sometimes, it really was worth it to stand up for what you believe in. Everyone who worked for a living was entitled to a prosperous life.

As of the time of this writing, I am still on disability from the Cook County Sheriffs Department under the care of two doctors and going through the classified ads every day, in the hopes of finding another job.

Over the period of the last five years, I'd seen many things at the jail: some good, some not so good. All of it had been a learning experience though.

Inmates come and go from the county jail, officers come and go, brass members get transferred from one division to the next, but the one thing that never seemed to change was the attitude of the administrative staff. The I-don't-give-a-damn attitude was there when I arrived, and it will be there long after I leave. That's just the way the county is.

The inmates detained at the jail were there for many different types of crimes: murder, rape, robbery, child molestation, drug dealing, arson, manslaughter, theft, attempted murder, gang activities, and numerous other offenses. Very few of the inmates ever learned from their mistakes the first time around. Many of them came back time after time and still didn't change their lives. It really didn't help that some of the officers, medical staff, and civilians working at the jail were breaking the law too.

For every good officer who worked at the county jail there were at least three bad ones. For every inmate who came through the system and was found innocent, there were at least a dozen more who were found guilty. The odds were not good at all!

As with people, jobs, inmates, and civilians, there is good and bad in everyone and everything in the world. We just need to find the good and concentrate on making it stronger.

The Cook County Jail was a holding facility for inmates awaiting trials and sentencings. If they were convicted, with all the things that go on here, I can just imagine what it would be like to work for one of the state penitentiaries, holding inmates who had been given life sentences or the death penalty.

ABOUT THE AUTHOR

C.J. Wilkinson is originally from Chicago, IL. and now resides in Tennessee. She loves horseback riding and writing poetry. She has a husband of thirteen years and two boys: Derald Jr. and Cameron, as well as three grandchildren: Daman Lamar, Katelyn, and Tyler James. She enjoys spending time with her three dogs and one cat.

CPSIA information can be obtained
at www.ICGtesting.com
Printed in the USA
LVHW050124060619
620305LV00001B/31/P